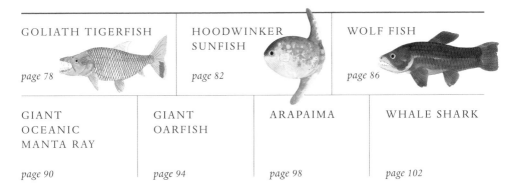
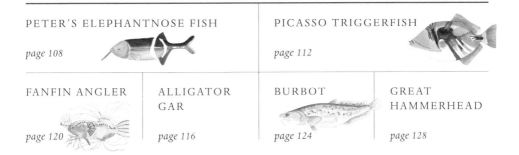
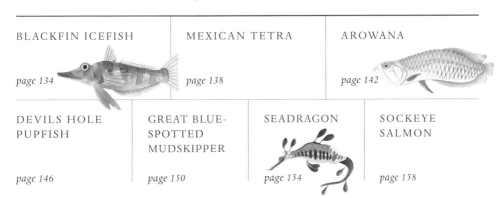

Chapter 6 LEGENDS OF OLD

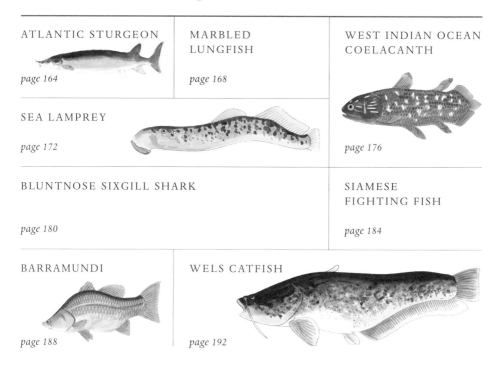
Chapter 7 WORLD TRAVELERS

Foreword

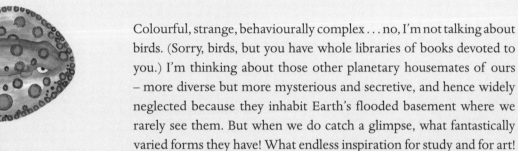

Colourful, strange, behaviourally complex . . . no, I'm not talking about birds. (Sorry, birds, but you have whole libraries of books devoted to you.) I'm thinking about those other planetary housemates of ours – more diverse but more mysterious and secretive, and hence widely neglected because they inhabit Earth's flooded basement where we rarely see them. But when we do catch a glimpse, what fantastically varied forms they have! What endless inspiration for study and for art!

Which makes this book such a pleasure for me: fish can be seen swimming across the pages on their way from the artist's mind to colonize other human minds. That is the place where, more than ever, they need to have a presence, not just because our ancestors came from the water (as did each of us, individually), but because we still depend on clean, healthy water. So paying attention to fish, and how well they are surviving, is at the very least a matter of self-interest.

And I'm particularly pleased to see freshwater fish so well represented here. Rivers and lakes hold a tiny fraction of the world's water (about 0.01 per cent) but fully half of all fish species. Much of this water is dark and cloudy, making its inhabitants hard to find and study. It's also why they're not as pretty as their flaunty cousins around coral reefs. But what they may lack in conventional good looks they make up for in weirdness and other ways . . .

Jump in and enjoy the swim!

Jeremy Wade

Presenter of *River Monsters* and *Mighty Rivers*, and official fish aficionado

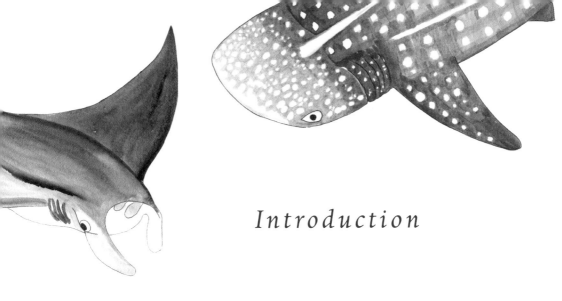

Introduction

There are more than 33,600 species of fish on this planet, which are grouped into approximately 515 families by taxonomists.

This book will introduce you to fifty distinctive fish species, each with its own remarkable story. Some you might be familiar with, but others might be completely new to you – however, they all represent just how important, amazing and intriguing fish can be.

The secrets of how their bodies work will be revealed – from their super-senses to their deadly toxins and their ability to give electric shocks. I will show you their strange and often baffling behaviours – explaining how and why they act as they do – and explore the history of how we came to discover their secrets. We'll see just how important a role they play in our lives and the world as a whole.

The fifty species featured live everywhere, from the deepest ocean to the shallowest pond, and take the form of giants the size of buses down to those no bigger than your thumb. All of them are important – and all of them reveal how amazing the natural world can be.

My accompanying illustrations are not especially scientifically accurate – they're more an attempt to capture the character of each fish. That said, they should still enable you to recognize each one if you come across it on your travels.

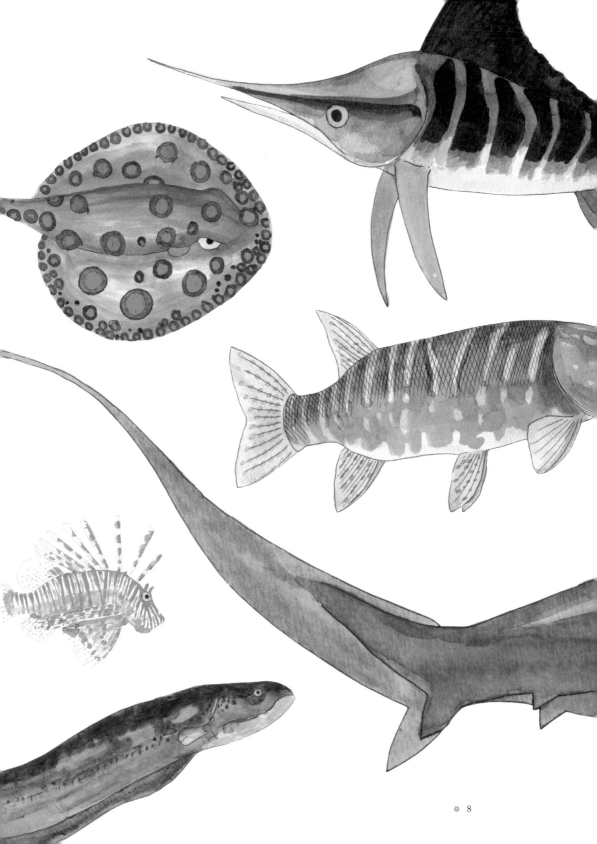

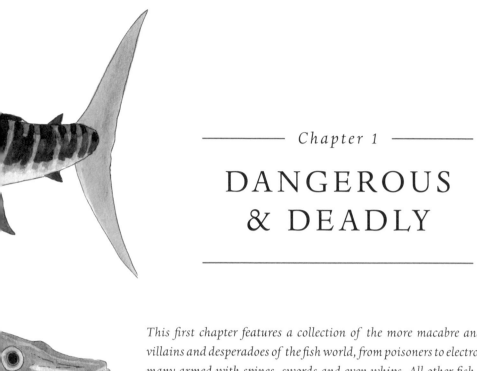

Chapter 1

DANGEROUS & DEADLY

This first chapter features a collection of the more macabre and despotic villains and desperadoes of the fish world, from poisoners to electrocutioners, many armed with spines, swords and even whips. All other fish need to be careful around these well-defended or viciously aggressive species, and some may even endanger humans. And although a few appear rather cute, all of them have a deadly secret up their sleeves.

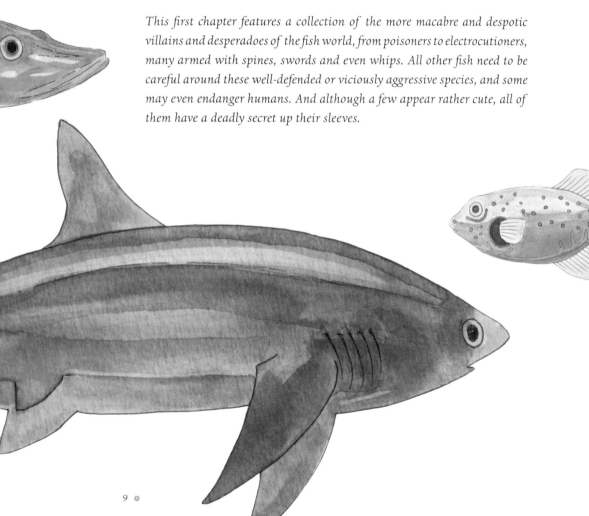

01

WHITE-SPOTTED PUFFER

{Arothron hispidus}

A.K.A.

Porcupinefish,
Tetraodon hispidus

SIZE

Up to 50 cm (20 in)

HABITAT

Reefs, lagoons,
estuaries and tidepools

**DISTINGUISHING
FEATURES**

Toothy

PERSONALITY

Solitary and defensive

LIKES

Sand sculptures

SPECIAL SKILLS

Highly toxic; can
inflate into a spiky ball

**CONSERVATION
STATUS**

Least Concern

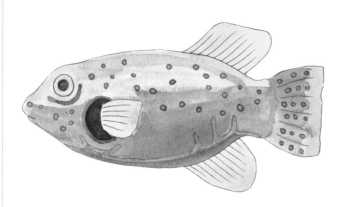

I COULD WRITE A whole book on these guys. There are more than 200 species of pufferfish in the family Tetraodontidae, which range from miniature freshwater versions the size of a thumb joint in India to giant African monsters; every species leads an elaborate and interesting life. There is a huge amount of variety in their patterns and shapes, but all of them can perform the same 'party trick', essential to their survival: when danger approaches, they can 'inflate' or 'puff' themselves into strange spiky balls.

They do this by taking in large amounts of water (or, if they are out of the water, air), expanding into their famous balloon shape by stretching their super-elastic skins. They can do this very rapidly, creating a startling defence mechanism that scares predators and can even make the pufferfish unpalatable. It's not usually the fish's first course of action, however; they will always try to swim away as fast as they can and conceal themselves first. If that doesn't work, then plan B comes into action: 'B' for 'blow up'!

This bizarre defence has a three-fold effect. Firstly, it takes any potential threat by surprise, startling it with speed and an unsettling shape and appearance (fish don't like being startled). Secondly, because the pufferfish is suddenly three times its initial size, they quickly become huge. Before, they just looked like little edible snacks, but now they may not even fit into a potential predator's mouth. Lastly, many species of pufferfish are covered in protective spines – some so much so that they are called 'porcupinefish'.

It is a unique and dramatic defensive tactic, but in many ways it's also a little over the top as pufferfish are also among the most toxic creatures on the planet. If a predator swallows it, it can die, which is too late for the pufferfish, as it will also be dead. So the process of inflating into a frightening spiny ball means that the predator can learn the lesson not to eat a puffer without killing either itself or its intended prey. Despite this, there is no shortage of potential threats: sharks, dolphins and other large ocean dwellers are all known to eat pufferfish and many seem immune to their prey's toxins. Eating a pufferfish can certainly kill us, but read the small print: it seems for some there are ways around this.

There are more than 200 species of pufferfish ... every species leads an elaborate and interesting life.

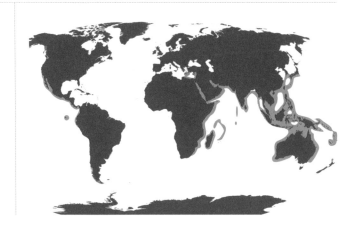

Poisonous poisson

The reason pufferfish are so deadly to many other creatures is due to the presence of a compound called tetrodotoxin (TTX) inside their bodies. This substance is 1,500 times more powerful, drop for drop, than cyanide. This deadly toxin is not produced by the fish themselves but derives from a bacteria that lives only in the bodies of pufferfish.

Despite knowing the dangers, humans still eat pufferfish. Known in Japan as *fugu*, they are a well-known delicacy, particularly when served in the sashimi style. Fugu chefs are trained for at least eleven years; the apprenticeship alone lasts for three years. The key to *fugu* preparation lies in the fact that TTX is only found in certain parts of the fish's body, generally most concentrated in the liver, kidneys and sexual organs, although this varies from species to species, and there are often traces in their skin, particularly in younger fish. I have eaten *fugu* and it is really tasty – but I remain unconvinced that it is soooo tasty that I would run the risk of dying every time I ate it.

The largest member of the pufferfish family is the mbu puffer (*Tetraodon mbu*) – a freshwater species. It can grow to more than 75 cm (30 in) in length and blow itself up to the size of a soccer ball. It is found in a band across the rivers and lakes of central Africa from the Congo to Lake Tanganyika. The mbu puffer is just as poisonous as some of the marine species and there is no known antitoxin.

If inflated with water, they can deflate in seconds. If it's air, then it's a little more complicated.

Four front teeth

Their family name, Tetraodontidae, has nothing to do with their toxin – rather, the toxin is named after the family – but everything to do with their teeth. Puffers have four prominent front teeth (*tetra* meaning 'four' and *odont* meaning 'tooth' in ancient Greek) that are almost fused, so that even if you look at one closely, it resembles a beak. This adaptation means that they can focus on some foods that are out of reach of other fish, such as snails, crustaceans and coral. Puffers can break up the calcareous defences of their prey efficiently using this parrot-like tool and the success of this winning design has taken the family into seas, rivers, lakes and estuaries all over the tropics and beyond.

One species of pufferfish could be described as an 'artist'. Off the coast of Japan, the diminutive love-lorn male of a creature going by the confusingly similar name of white-spotted pufferfish (*Torquigener albomaculosus*) creates something unique. So remarkable are its achievements that, when first revealed by divers in 1995, no one had any idea what had made them. They discovered vast and intricate spherical patterns in the sand, measuring more than 2 m (7 ft) in diameter and looking rather more like something out of science fiction than a fish nest, which is what they turned out to be.

No one had any idea what had made them.

Despite the rumours of the constructions being built by aliens or pranksters (in a similar way to the crop circles that appeared in Britain in the 1980s), it took almost twenty years before the true culprit was identified and published in a scientific paper, having been caught in mid-build. The mysterious architect was a small, 12-cm (5-in), rather dull-looking (or, more accurately, well-camouflaged) male pufferfish of a species new to science. Its patterns took up to six weeks to construct and were all made using just fins, endurance and the drive to reproduce, with all these labours being performed to woo a female. Clearly, even the most toxic fish have more to them than meets the eye. So can I now sign you up to the Puffer Appreciation Society?

02

STRIPED MARLIN

{Kajikia audax}

A.K.A.

Marlin, billfish, 'stripey'

SIZE

Up to 3.7 m (12 ft)

HABITAT

Pacific and Indian Oceans

DISTINGUISHING FEATURES

A sword for a nose

PERSONALITY

High-speed wanderlust

LIKES

Shoals of baitfish

SPECIAL SKILLS

Speed and manoeuvrability

CONSERVATION STATUS

Near Threatened

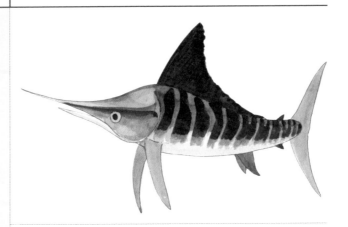

WHO WOULDN'T WANT a sword for a nose? It is the most elegant and extraordinary way to cut through the water. I mean, not even the best artificial intelligence inventors on earth could create a creature that just looks and moves like one of these perfect oceanic fish – they are impossible to misidentify. However, there is a reason I've placed them in the 'Dangerous & Deadly' chapter and that's because they are one of the apex predators of the open ocean.

Even though they are the smallest of the marlin or billfish family Istiophoridae – of which there are eleven species – the striped marlin is massive, reaching lengths of 3.7 m (12 ft) and can weigh in at 204 kg (450 lb). They are dynamic, taut barrels of energy with adjustable fins that act like aquafoils, being raised or dropped

They are one of the apex predators of the open ocean.

to different angles depending on which speed may be needed. This similarity to a motor yacht gives marlins a further alternative name, that of sailfish, though there are two other species in the family in the genus *Istiophorus* that are more correctly termed sailfish. These huge, sharply pointed pectoral fins direct and steer them at high speeds, so they can pirouette and spin, while wielding that immense sword-like snout like an expert fencer, slashing and parrying shoals of silvery, shiny baitfish, slicing and stunning them to be gulped down quickly. These finely tuned, turbocharged adaptations put them in line with the fastest animals in the oceans, along with other top sprinters such the mako sharks and tuna family, of which more later (see pages 202–5).

Zebra striped

The striped marlin is the most widely distributed of the billfish family and perhaps the most beautiful with those Gucci stripes and dazzling blue and black colouration. Other marlin species are mostly restricted to the world's tropical seas but 'stripeys' (as I like to call them) are somewhat more hardy and venture into subtropical and even some temperate waters. The species is highly migratory, following shoals of baitfish wherever they lead them. Consequently, a fish cruising around the Gulf of Mexico one day could be scything through the waves off New Caledonia a few weeks later. These fish can travel thousands of miles over several days and are incredibly hard to pin down. They are found throughout the Indo-Pacific Ocean – in fact, the only place they aren't generally found is in the Atlantic – and, although mostly solitary, striped marlin can form big colourful shoals concentrated in large areas of open water, which can make fishing easy for the knowledgeable angler. One of the best places to see them is off the coast of Baja California, where the deep but clear blue waters show them off at their best.

The biggest problem with being fast, energetic and ubiquitous is that marlin naturally draw the attention of the most dangerous and effective predators on Earth: humans. To make matters worse, their oxygen-rich, high-speed lives make their meat red, rich and, according to many, delicious. Unsurprisingly, striped marlin have become a favourite target for unsustainable harvesting, with twenty-three large fisheries dedicated to catching this species alone. Its world and local populations have come under immense hunting pressures: according to the Billfish Working Group, the weight of striped marlin caught in 1975 was an immense 18,739 tons (17,000 tonnes) but, by 2016, that number had fallen to a mere 6,614 tons (6,000 tonnes). That wasn't because of a decision by the industry to catch less fish, but because the numbers of striped marlin had fallen so drastically.

Shoaling fish are right to look worried when a marlin turns up.

Cryptic ocean nomad

Such a parlous state isn't merely due to the species' wanderlust but also that there is much about its life we don't know. We are quite ignorant about how long they live, major parts of their life cycle, how quickly they grow or the age at which they become sexually mature. Scientific evidence suggests they grow quickly in their first two years, but we have little idea of what happens afterwards, and so much of their lives remains shrouded in mystery.

This lack of knowledge makes the fish's long-term management and conservation incredibly hard. Balancing the nutritional and recreational requirements of humans while maintaining the species' numbers at a healthy level is a mammoth and complex task. The big question is how can we manage striped marlin to supply the insatiable global market and leave enough in the wild to sustain a healthy breeding population – one that is large enough to withstand all the other trials that nature throws at them, including disease or bad breeding seasons, for generations to come?

> *The big question is how can we manage striped marlin to supply the insatiable global market and leave enough in the wild.*

So how can we manage a species' survival when we don't really understand its lifestyle and life history? Many biologists are working round the clock to find this information out; let's hope they succeed before striped marlin disappear because of overfishing!

Let's also take a moment to consider the beauty and wonder of these amazing fish. Whether you call them swordfish, marlin or billfish, they are impressive and sleek, oceanic super-machines, but when they hatch from their small floating eggs, they are anything but streamlined; baby marlin must be some of the goofiest baby creatures on the planet, perhaps even giving the ocean sunfish (*Mola mola*) a run for their money (see pages 82–5).

03

RED LIONFISH

{Pterois volitans}

A.K.A.

Zebrafish, firefish, turkeyfish, butterfly cod, scorpion volitans

SIZE

40 cm (15 in)

HABITAT

Inshore waters and aquaria

DISTINGUISHING FEATURES

Long fins and poisonous spines

PERSONALITY

Ruthless predator

LIKES

Fighting

SPECIAL SKILLS

A venomous sting

CONSERVATION STATUS

Least Concern

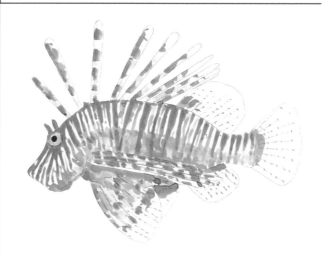

T HERE ARE FEW fish as beautiful (or as complicated to paint) as the red lionfish. Their flowing, candy-striped, filamentous fins make them look like a spectacular submarine armada. They are also heavily armed with spines, and this weaponry, coupled with an appetite of a wrestler, combine to form a truly ferocious predator. Lionfish are the pirates of the fish world, wreaking havoc throughout the Caribbean.

The lionfish genus (*Pterois*) is native to the Indo-Pacific Ocean, and the fish are mostly found inshore, favouring reefs and harbours, but they've claimed victims as far away as Chicago, more than 2,000 km (1,423 miles) from the sea.

In one year, an estimated 30,000 lionfish were imported into the United States.

A lion in the tank

With their exotic beauty, lionfish have fast become some of the most in-demand aquarium fish on the planet. In one year, between April 2016–2017, an estimated 30,000 lionfish were imported into the United States. The problem is that they often outgrow their tanks, eat all the other living creatures they shared it with and put their owners in hospital (an expensive proposition in the United States).

Tucked away among all that razzmatazz of fins and finery are eighteen hidden spines, which are sharp enough to puncture even the toughest of skins. The fish then injects a nasty venom into its perceived assailant. The most dangerous fins are arrayed throughout the dorsal fins (those found on the top) – there are thirteen in total concealed among all the flamboyance and one more on each pelvic fin – and three in the anal fin. Trying to fit a whole lionfish in its mouth is a mistake a predator only makes once. A lionfish will erect all of its fins and, under even the slightest pressure, the fin's sheath will push back to reveal a stabbing spine, shooting venom through grooves along its length to poison its foe, often the last thing the latter ever experiences.

Toxic shock

Lionfish venom contains acetylcholine, the chemical that humans have in their body to help move muscles. In concentrated quantities, acetylcholine is a neurotransmitter, allowing the nerves to feel a pain described as more excruciating than almost anything else imaginable, usually accompanied by swelling, bleeding and bruising, and if you're lucky, some numbness. You aren't likely to die, but anaphylactic shock due to allergy, cardiac arrest, fainting and shortness of breath are all possible. Medical attention should be sought.

Sometimes there is an 'outbreak' of lionfish envenomations, and this happened in Chicago over a period of two years between 1993–1994 when thirty-three people were treated in an emergency centre for lionfish sting injuries to the hand, though only two were hospitalized. Though lionfish are marine species, some inland ER staff in Chicago have become experts in dealing with such injuries, owing to the mishandling of the fish by those keeping them in aquariums. Why are these injuries so common? Lionfish are known to be highly territorial and very aggressive. So when an intrusive hand comes into view, they are likely to 'accidentally on purpose' home in on the intruder.

Lionfish invasion

The danger of this fish species has also become apparent as it has established itself as an invasive species in Florida, first being noted in 1985 on the Atlantic coast at Dania Beach. This was the beginning of a full-scale invasion. In 2019, a two-day lionfish-collecting festival in the state, participants managed to catch a total of 15,000 lionfish. Red lionfish has fast established itself off much of the Atlantic coast of America as far north as North Carolina and around the Caribbean.

Lionfish can lay thousands upon thousands of eggs throughout the year.

As we become ever more aware of how ecosystems work, we know that introducing an apex predator into a world that can't defend itself against their depredations tends not to end well. Lionfish are now thriving in the warmer waters of the Atlantic and the Gulf of Mexico, reducing the populations of native fish and competing with native predators such as groupers and snappers, thus upsetting the

These fish are no shrinking violets – they are quite often easy to see.

balance of these well-established ecosystems.

The biggest concern is that lionfish not only prey on fish that have no known defences against them but also target fish species that play a vital role in that ecosystem – such as eating algae or removing over-populated crustaceans. Once a particular species has been removed or inhibited enough to be unable to fulfil its role, the whole ecosystem can collapse. Regular lionfish clean-ups are organized in Florida, Aruba and other affected locations by individuals and dive schools, with divers taking the sport of hunting the fish very enthusiastically, though it's unlikely that permanent eradication will ever be achieved. There is one big advantage to hunting lionfish: they are reputedly delicious. If you are in the Caribbean or Florida and order lionfish in a restaurant, you will be saving the environment – something that can't be said of many fish species on menus!

Lionfish are ruthless predators that roam the reefs all day and night without needing to be fearful of any larger creature attempting to eat them. They can control the levels of air in their swim bladders (the sac filled with oxygen, which enables fish to maintain buoyancy without floating or sinking). This enables lionfish to move around almost without any other physical effort, with their fins splayed and fanned out, dazing and confusing their prey before they are consumed. When breeding, lionfish can lay thousands upon thousands of eggs throughout the year.

Fortunately, in their native habitats, lionfish numbers are kept in check by the different species of predators, including sharks that hunt them. But because lionfish are not native to the Caribbean, the sharks there are unfamiliar with them and do not recognize lionfish as food. So to control their numbers, marine biologists are trying to train sharks to eat them – in other words, enlisting a fish to help control the invasion. Although it's going to take time before an impact is made on this environmental disaster, let's keep our fingers crossed and hope those Caribbean sharks are hungry.

04

NORTHERN PIKE

{Esox lucius}

A.K.A.

Jack, luce, pike-fish

SIZE

On average 25–63 cm
(10–25 in)

HABITAT

Streams, lakes and
large rivers

**DISTINGUISHING
FEATURES**

Stripes and teeth

PERSONALITY

Lurker

LIKES

Eats almost anything

SPECIAL SKILLS

Staying perfectly still
before attacking

**CONSERVATION
STATUS**

Least Concern

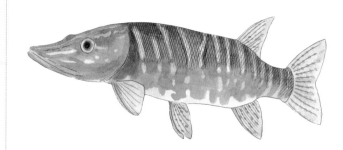

THERE ARE FEW more terrifying predators than the secretive and vicious northern pike. Most fish don't even get the chance to swim away – it's all over for them in a flurry of scales, bubbles and a gaping, jagged mouth full of dagger-like teeth. Even if the prey does escape with a flesh wound, pike saliva has an anticoagulant in it to prevent the poor victim's blood from congealing, which means it could bleed out.

Northern pike closely resembles the ocean-going barracuda, though it is completely unrelated to this genus of marine fish. It has low, under-slung jaws, is torpedo-shaped and uses its rear fins to power along and to produce 'explosions' of fast, dynamic action. Northern pike is the largest freshwater predatory fish across Europe and Canada and North America, not to be confused with the very similar pike species called the muskellunge (*E. masquinongy*) found in North America. 'Muskies' (or, indeed, 'lunges') are a little larger than northern pike but have a much more limited distribution. Hybrids are well known between muskies and northern pike, and are rather beautiful; they are commonly referred to as 'tiger pike' but are sterile and often bred in captivity for the benefit of anglers, then released into controlled fisheries or private rivers and lakes, from where they escape into the wild.

Mammoth pike

The largest-ever northern pike on record was a 25-kg (55-lb) monster in Germany, caught in 1986. Of course, fishermen always tell stories of larger 'ones that got away' and reports of larger pike abound, with reports of fish weighing 31 kg (68 lb) and measuring 1.5 m (58 in) long, and 35 kg (77 lb) measuring 1.8 m (72 in) to be found in the angling literature. However, the final word has to go to angling historian Fred Buller and his *Domesday Book of Mammoth Pike*, which has even bigger fish listed, though these are not considered fully documented in a modern sense.

If a truly big pike is seen, then it is highly likely to be a female. Female northern pike considerably outsize the males, and it is usually the most reliable way to tell the genders apart. During spring, when the water is high, amorous pike head to the weedier areas of their underwater territories. The breeding imperative means that the males' usual wariness is put aside. They nudge and buffet the female, encouraging her to release the eggs into the weeds below. This is the trigger for

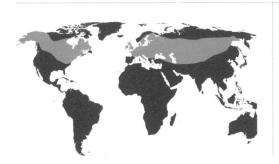

If a truly big pike is seen, then it is highly likely to be a female.

all the males to fertilize them simultaneously with a cloud of milt (actually their sperm, which then proceed to compete with each other and the strongest makes it to the egg). Thousands of sticky, fertilized eggs attach to the surrounding vegetation and hatch within two weeks into tiny, tiger-striped pikelets.

Those jaws are designed for one thing only: grabbing.

Not so northern

Northern pike can live in a range of climatic regions, from the warm French Riviera to the harsh winters of Siberia, even where the water surface above has frozen. Anglers drill through such ice – which can be metres thick in places – to lower lures with the purpose of tantalizing hungry pike. Ice fishing for pike has a magical attraction for many fishermen and there is a lot of footage available on the internet, with pike even filmed underwater watching dancing lures, ready to snap at them. More essentially, northern pike plays an important role in native peoples' diets in the frozen north of Scandinavia and America.

Northern pike is highly territorial, with the biggest fish dominating and younger, smaller pike, known as 'jack pike', being somewhat warier. However, jack are more aesthetically pleasing, which is why my illustration is of one. As pike grow, those bright yellow bands fade away to reveal a more consistant olive colouration. Their camouflage is essential when youngsters, as larger pike are notorious for being cannibals. And it's said that if you remove the largest pike from a lake, all hell breaks loose among the smaller 'jacks' as they try to eat each other to get as big as possible in order to rule their watery kingdom. Jack pike are pugnacious and precocious – often with 'eyes too big for their bellies'; they have occasionally been found choked to death trying to swallow individuals of their own kind and as big as themselves.

Brutal elegance

The brutality of the species' upbringing is belied by its clear elegance. Those large pectoral and dorsal fins allow the fish to hover in the water, using minor adjustments in the speed and shape of its fins to sustain a still position almost supernaturally; it appears to almost be hanging on a wire. This elegance has a darker side: the incredible sense of balance allows the fish to be deadly accurate and precise when striking at any would-be meal. Though seemingly frozen still, the pike is in a state almost redolent of a coiled spring before it surges forwards, like a sprinter after the starting pistol. As it lunges, it turns its massive head rapidly to one side to snatch its prey in its cavernous, almost crocodile-like jaws. Backward-facing, sharply pointed teeth prevent the prey's escape once it is grabbed. These fangs make removing a fishing hook from its mouth something to be done with great care and attention.

Small prey is usually despatched at the moment of capture, but bigger creatures can be drowned and then shaken apart (again, somewhat in the manner of a crocodile). Pike are fairly indiscriminate eaters, taking most fish species, along with frogs, small mammals (mice, rats and voles often take to the water) and birds (especially the more helpless chicks); there are apocryphal reports of the occasional dog going missing due to large pike, though these remain unsubstantiated.

The large pectoral and dorsal fins allow the fish to hover in the water.

There are a few reports – again, unproven – of the odd person sustaining an unprovoked attack (rather than during hook removal), including a couple of dubious reports from Victorian England, although that was more likely propaganda to encourage pike removal from the landed gentry's trout waters or from fish farms. In fact, pike and brown trout (see pages 198–201) are often found in the same lakes and rivers and can live quite happily side by side in the wild. So although pike are just the most perfect predator, they are also, like many apex predators, the guardians of their ecosystems – keeping them strong and healthy – and should be respected for it.

05

OCELLATE RIVER STINGRAY

{*Potamotrygon motoro*}

A.K.A.

Motoro stingray, black river stingray

SIZE

50–60 cm (20–24 in)

HABITAT

Shallow muddy water

DISTINGUISHING FEATURES

Concealed samurai sword in the tail

PERSONALITY

Patient hunter

LIKES

Crustaceans and other fish

SPECIAL SKILLS

Camouflage and ambush

CONSERVATION STATUS

Insufficient data

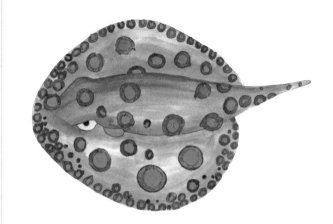

It's exciting enough that stingrays can be found the sea, but they also live in rivers. Despite the presence of piranhas and wolf fish, this is the fish that most South American indigenous people are really scared of; all of them will, at some point, have been hurt by one of these secretive, elusive but dangerous rays.

Ocellate river (also known as motoro or black river) stingrays have evolved specifically not to be seen – a fact that is most unfortunate for people wading in shallow muddy water in bare feet within the fish's range. Though not usually fatal, first-hand accounts of freshwater stingray stings say the pain is like no other, often made worse by dirty water causing secondary infections if injuries are not quickly and carefully treated.

How does this flat geeky-looking thing pack such a punch? And where does it keep all this weaponry? The secret lies in its long, thin tail. While there are many different types of stingray in the world, it's the Potamotrygonidae that are the most dangerous. Every one of the thirty-eight species (solely found in South America, though there is another similar family, Dasyatidae, found in Africa and Asia) has a sheath hidden along the top of their tails containing a blade like a very small samurai sword edged with thousands of tiny barbs. When threatened or trodden on, the fish turns its tail back on itself and slashes at the perceived threat. This weaponry is purely designed for self-defence and is highly potent and functional.

Stinging simplicity

The entire mechanism is fairly unsophisticated. The barbed stinger rests inside the sheath in a pool of venom and mucus, immersing the blade continuously. As this slashes you around the ankles or shins, some of that sticky venom will inevitably find its way into your system via the open wounds created by the edge of the fish's blade. This traumatic process can be likened to being slashed with a rusty, infected serrated bread knife – there is almost always plenty of blood and the venom-ridden goo will usually get into you. It's not elegant – but it is effective.

If you are unfortunate enough to find yourself wounded by a freshwater stingray, it is best to calmly exit the water (as calmly as you can in intense pain!) and wash the wound with the most 'sterile

This is the fish that most South American indigenous people are really scared of.

solution' you can find as soon as possible; warm, soapy water is best, but if this is not available, then the purest alcohol possible can be used – it is sterile but will hurt like hell, though not as much as the actual stingray sting. The water or alcohol will wash away any residual venom. Placing the injury into hot water may also help, though ensure this is not scalding; leave it submerged for as long as you can; in the meantime, seek medical attention.

The fish can lie in wait for many hours, days or weeks.

Cleaning the wound thoroughly is especially important as parts of the stinger can sometimes break off inside the wound, causing secondary infections and even more unpleasantness. Perhaps unfairly, the act of stinging leaves the stingray largely unaffected, and even if the whole stinger snaps off, it can grow back within a few weeks; although this is unlikely a comfort if you have pieces of it inside you.

Stingray ambush

Ocellate river stingrays, however, do not just exist to create injury and danger for unwary passing humans and other animals – they are expert ambush predators. Finding an area of soft mud, stony riverbed or lakebed in the shallows, they wave their amazing, wing-like fins, digging down into the substrate and throwing dirt, gravel and sediment over their backs. The species' colourful, blotchy brown pattern is fun to paint but also one of the best camouflages to be found in nature; even when you know the species is present right in front of you, it is almost impossible to see. The only likely giveaway is the fish's gill – which is more like a protruding tube (the area just behind the eye it is inflated and deflated as the fish breathes, subtly revealing the fish's whereabouts). Once buried in position, the fish can lie in wait for many hours, days or even weeks, if necessary; whether the individual fish occasionally moves during this time is not known, but they are repeatedly found in exactly the same place. Once an appropriately sized item of prey swims past, the stingray erupts from its hiding place to snatch the unfortunate

The underneath of a ray is not nearly as colourful as the top.

victim, that is, unless an unfortunate person almost treads on it first; either way, something is getting hurt!

The Potamotrygonidae are a bit of an anomaly; it is known that, way back in the Eocene period (around 50 million years ago, when early rhinoceroses were evolving and the Himalayas were only just rising), much of South America was underwater. As the waters receded, they left behind a large number of marine species. Of course, it took a long time for the sea to recede entirely, so some of these species had the chance to adapt to the new, fresher water surroundings (freshwater dolphin and manatee species also underwent the same prolonged process).

More recent research discoveries have shown that the stingrays' beautiful and colourful characteristics vary with their toxicity as they mature. Youngsters' stings merely cause pain, but the wounds from an older fish can cause necrosis – which is the actual death of cells or tissue. A better understanding of how these dangerous creatures behave is essential to reduce the injuries caused, but the process of how their venom works is also fascinating; we may even be able to turn it to our advantage in the way that cobra snake venom has been used to treat high blood pressure for many years. And rather than see the fish as something to fear but rather something to learn from we may soon be saving more lives than they have ever harmed.

06

COMMON THRESHER

{Alopias vulpinus}

A.K.A.

Sea fox, swiveltail, thrasher

SIZE

Up to 6 m (20 ft)

HABITAT

Temperate waters

DISTINGUISHING FEATURES

A tail as long as its body

PERSONALITY

Solitary traveller

LIKES

Whole shoals of fish

SPECIAL SKILLS

Can jump right out of the water

CONSERVATION STATUS

Endangered

THRESHERS WERE ALWAYS my favourite kind of shark when growing up. While bull sharks were impressive and able to swim up rivers, tiger sharks were powerful and could bite through turtle shells and great white sharks were astonishingly large and legendary via the movie *Jaws*, it was the bizarre shape and mystery of the huge, alien-looking tail of threshers that beguiled me.

Threshers can measure 6 m (20 ft) in length, which might seem huge until you realize that the shark's tail can account for half of the animal's body length. A common thresher's tail is approximately as long as its body and serves purposes which are still being uncovered by biologists. Historically, experts have theorized that the sharks used their tails to catch food. However, no one appears to have ever seen them do it, partly owing to the difficulties in finding and observing them in the wild. There are even unlikely ancient mariners' tales suggesting that threshers and swordfish team up to catch whales: while the threshers stir the water in front of a whale into a froth with their long tails to confuse the sea mammals, the swordfish stab the creatures with their noses, ultimately killing them and allowing both fish to feast together. The trouble with this story – along with the lack of observation and overall unlikelihood – is that there is not even any circumstantial biological evidence for it, let alone that a thresher's teeth are not close to being designed in a way to successfully bite into whales.

Whipped into shape

However, in 2013, a scientific team off the coast of the Philippines (a region favoured by large numbers of threshers) witnessed the shark's elongated rear appendage in action. It turned out that it was, indeed, used for hunting, but that there were two different attack strategies. Firstly, a 'ball' of fish was located (usually made up of sardines, anchovies or other kinds of baitfish that love to form huge shoals); these smaller fish form spherical shoals when under threat from predators, a shape that leaves less fish vulnerable and accessible to the predators. Thresher Attack Plan 1 involves a frontal assault: the shark swims super-fast towards the bait ball and then, at the last second, slams on the brakes using its large pectoral fins. In the same instant, it drops its head, bringing its tail lashing over the top to smash into

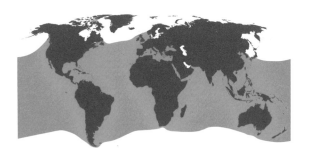

A common thresher's tail is approximately as long as its body.

the shoal like a massive horsewhip. Thresher Attack Plan 2 involves a slight variation where it turns at the last minute so that its tail lashes out at the side instead. Both techniques seem to be very effective.

The powerful whipping effect of the shark's tail stuns or even kills many individual prey fish, allowing the thresher to clear the bodies up and feast at leisure. This sledgehammer method has the advantage of allowing the shark to consume more fish in one hunt than it would by hunting more conventionally. These threshers can deliver the 'whack' with such speed that, via rapid diffusion, it even forces carbon dioxide out of the water, creating a fizz of bubbles that also add to all the confusion.

The powerful whipping effect of the shark's tail can stun or even kill.

The word 'thresher' comes from the ancient process of pounding wheat to separate the ears of corn from the stalks. Before the process was industrialized, threshing was performed using hand-held flails, which resembled the shark's long tail fluke. Such flails were also used as weapons and are the origin of the more modern *nunchaku*, familiar from 'kung fu' films and used in several Asian martial arts disciplines.

Wily threshers

Surprisingly, this remarkable appendage was not the prominent detail that was noticed when the thresher was first scientifically described. Initially, this odd shark species was officially named in the eighteenth century by a Frenchman called Bonnaterre, who gave it the original scientific name *Squalus vulpines* – which roughly translates as 'fox-like shark', resulting in its common name being 'fox shark' for many years after. This not-so-obvious nomenclature came from the shark being supposedly cunning and clever in its hunting habits – attributes traditionally levelled at the character of a wild fox.

Latin names are often subject to change – albeit it slowly – and threshers were eventually moved into their own family, the Alopiidae (also derived from ancient Greek for 'fox' – it wasn't going to shake

With that tail, there is no mistaking this shark.

that idea off for some time, it seems), which is now home to three species: the common thresher, the big-eye thresher (*A. superciliosus*) and, most recently, in 1935, the pelagic thresher (*A. pelagicus*). All have their slight differences in colouration and habits, but all are discernible by that extended tail, as long as their bodies.

To see a thresher, you don't even have to be underwater; the thresher is one of the few sharks that launches its entire body out of the water. That whip-like tail is not only used to herd smaller fish to their doom but is also able to propel the shark at enormous speed when necessary. This spectacular behaviour, made famous by the great white shark but other animals do it too, like penguins, seals, dolphins and whales, is called 'breaching'; to achieve it, thresher sharks reach speeds of up to 65 kph (40 mph) and can clear the ocean surface by around 3 m (10 ft). It can happen when the sharks are hunting, but it is also believed they might do it to rid themselves of skin parasites. Personally I wouldn't need a reason, I would just do it because I could – all the time.

07

ELECTRIC EEL

{*Electrophorus electricus*}

A.K.A.

Knifefish

SIZE

Up to 2.5 m (8 ft)

HABITAT

The bottom of muddy swamps

DISTINGUISHING FEATURES

No scales, three electrical organs

PERSONALITY

Shocking

LIKES

Hunting at night

SPECIAL SKILLS

Can produce up to 850 volts

CONSERVATION STATUS

Least Concern

L ET'S START BY getting something glaringly obvious out of the way first. Despite its name, the electric eel is not an eel at all but a species of knifefish found solely in South America, like the rest of its group. Its classification as a knifefish has only been relatively recently revised, but first impressions sometimes count, as no less a taxonomist than the Swedish originator of the binomial system, Carl Linnaeus, originally classified them in the same genus as banded knifefish (*Gymnotus carapo*) in 1766. So it has taken a long time for them to return to their rightful evolutionary position.

There have been other changes afoot concerning this intriguing 'species'. There are now understood to be three species of electric eel, not one, all of which are capable of administering the electric shock they are famous for, but each produces a greater or lesser amount of charge than the others.

E. voltai *can pump out a staggering maximum of 850 volts.*

From a tickle to a shock

The most common species was the one originally described by Linnaeus, *Electrophorus electricus*, which can generate an electrical charge of 600 volts, tops. The gentlest of the three is *E. vari*, which produces a maximum of 150 volts (with the effect of a gentle electrical tickle), while the most shocking is *E. voltai*, which can pump out a staggering maximum of 850 volts.

All three species of electric eel are large and visually similar – they can grow up to 2.5 m (8 ft) in length and can be as thick as a mountain-bike tyre. They are found exclusively in the rivers of South America, from Panama, throughout Amazonia, to the Atlantic and as far south as Argentina. They produce the highest electrical charge of any living creature on the planet. Although how much charge at any one time varies between species and individuals, as we have seen, but also depends on what the eel is up to.

The amount of current discharged depends upon the task at hand. If an 'eel' is just on the lookout for a hole to hide in for the day, it produces a low electrical charge, which it uses like sonar to navigate through murky water, in a similar way that a bat uses sound to 'see' in the dark. However, if, say, a giant otter attempts to grab it, then a full power supply can be dramatically administered in one tremendous pulse. This flexibility of discharge is one of the reasons it has taken biologists so long to identify the separate species, making you wonder what other discoveries are still out there to be uncovered.

Humboldt and the horses

The indigenous Amazonian people have been living with the eels for 40,000 years or so, but one of the first 'Westerners' to come across them was the Prussian explorer Alexander von Humboldt in March 1800. Having been told that there was a lake nearby full of electric eels, he asked the locals to collect some for him. This may have seemed an eccentric demand, as the locals preferred avoiding them to catching them. Even so, the well-travelled Humboldt was a little surprised by local hunting methods, which involved driving some wild horses into the big muddy lake, rather than nets, rods and hooks.

Electric eels produce the highest electrical charge of any living creature on the planet.

What then happened was astounding. In seconds, the water looked as if it was boiling with thrashing bodies, and Humboldt witnessed several eels lifting themselves out of the water and pressing their entire bodies directly against the horses' stomachs, pulsing with charge. After a few minutes of this assault, however, the eels tumbled back into the churning water. Only then did the men enter the water to collect the exhausted but still alive eels. The horses appeared to survive – minus a couple that Humboldt assumed had succumbed to the stampede and drowned rather than died of electric shock.

Humboldt's dramatic account became well known, but no one appeared to have ever seen electric eels attack in this way since. The story remained a piece of biological legend, until 2019, when Kenneth Catiana, a student from Vanderbilt University, Tennessee, USA, filmed some extraordinary behaviour among captive electric eels under laboratory conditions. He used a fake caiman head instead of a living horse and introduced it into an aquarium housing an eel. It certainly didn't disappoint. The eel proactively assaulted the intruder in exactly the same way that Humboldt witnessed – riding right along the length of the caiman head and lighting up LEDs that had been set up on the prosthetic. Proving not only that the explorer's account had been correct but that it is also unwise to upset an electric eel.

Internal generator

How do the eels create these huge electrical charges? In fact, all animals and plants generate electricity. Human muscles and nerves are all driven by electrical pulses. However, electric eels have three organs dedicated to the production of concentrated electric charges. The 'main organ' on the fish's dorsal or top side starts just behind the head and runs along half of its body; Hunter's organ is located underneath on the ventral side; and Sachs' organ is at the fish's rear end. All three organs are made up of disc-like cells called electrocytes, which are stacked on top of one another like batteries in a torch. When the brain gives the order to attack via 'command nuclei' in the organs' cells, all simultaneously fire electricity. A single cell changes its potential difference using potassium ions, starting a chain reaction that generates a huge electrical pulse in the space of a few milliseconds. This charge is magnified by the action of water as a grounding medium. It is not yet known how the eels manage to avoid shocking themselves, but it may be something to do with the precision targeting of the electricity into adjacent smaller items, even if they are part of a larger object or animal.

It was interesting to be told an eyewitness story of electric eel hunting behaviour by a fisherman. One evening, he was watching an eel foraging in the shallows by the edge of a river. Suddenly, an entire shoal of sleeping fish all jumped out the water and landed, floating immobile, on the surface, as if they had been given a massive electric shock. The eel then slowly moved in and ate a couple of them before moving on. Remarkably, just a few seconds after the eel's departure, the remaining stunned fish shook themselves to life again and swam away, apparently unharmed. This demonstrates how even a fish, albeit one with awesome powers, manages to catch only what it needs.

Pores on the eel's skin help detect the faintest hint of electricity.

Chapter 2

MINIATURE MARVELS

While it may be tempting to be overly impressed by the largest and most fearsome in the world of fish, let's not forget the 'little 'uns'. These smaller species have just as an amazing and wonderful life as their bigger cousins. In this chapter, you will discover life-savers, light-bearers, Hollywood stars and one of the most infamous fish on Earth.

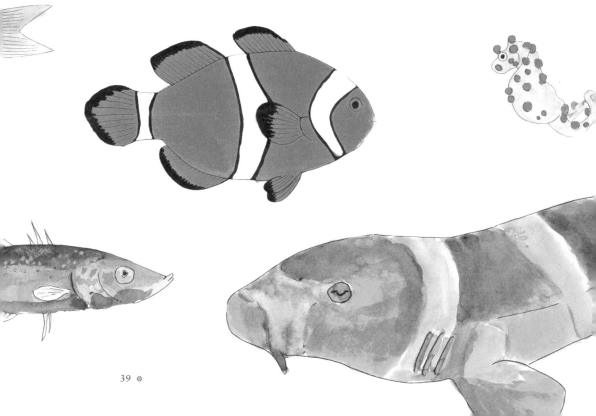

08

BARGIBANT'S PYGMY SEAHORSE

{Hippocampus bargibanti}

A.K.A.

Bargibant's seahorse

SIZE

Less than 2 cm (¾ in)

HABITAT

On fan corals

DISTINGUISHING FEATURES

Covered in knobbles that resemble the coral it hides in

PERSONALITY

Monogamous; males give birth

LIKES

Debris

SPECIAL SKILLS

Can evade detection

CONSERVATION STATUS

Insufficient data

WHILE THE WORD 'pygmy' is used to describe the smaller forms of many animals, it doesn't really help us judge exactly how much smaller that means. In the case of the eight species of pygmy seahorse, however, it means really tiny. Pygmy seahorses are among the smallest vertebrates to be found on the planet. So small are they that no one even knew to look for them, and they were discovered completely by accident.

One day in 1969, George Bargibant was collecting specimens for the Nouméa Museum in New Caledonia. He had acquired a large gorgonian sea fan of the genus *Muricella*. These are particularly spectacular forms of coral resembling a huge leaf skeleton, as can be seen in autumn and winter after the 'flesh' of the leaf has decayed. These giant free-standing corals are usually covered in small pink or orange polyps (the tentacled individual organisms that make up the colonial life-form we call a coral). As Bargibant was preparing a *Muricella* specimen for display, he noticed two very tiny seahorses on his laboratory table, which appeared to have fallen off the coral. He had inadvertently discovered a hitherto unknown species.

A large fan coral can have as many as twenty-eight pairs of Bargibant's pygmy seahorse living on them. These corals only grow to the size of a domestic rubber plant at best, so that is one seriously small stable and paddock for fifty-six minuscule horses.

Shrinking ponies

Of the other eight species of pygmy *Hippocampus* now described, the most recent, *H. nalu*, was found in South Africa and named and announced in May 2020. It is one of the larger species, reaching a stupendous 27 mm (1 1/16 in) at the most – not much larger than a big toenail. The Japanese pygmy seahorse (*H. japapigu*) was named in 2018 and is one of the smaller species, only reaching 16 mm (5/8 in). The Walea soft coral pygmy seahorse (*H. waleananus*) is restricted to the coasts off the island of Sulawesi, Indonesia and would be the smallest if it didn't have such a long tail to keep itself anchored around the thick stems of its coral habitat. Denise's pygmy seahorse (*H. denise*)

A pair of these little fish could sit comfortably on one key of a computer keyboard.

was described in 2003 from Wallacea (the island from Borneo to New Guinea) and lives on several different kinds of coral – including *Muricella* – in shallow water down to 90 m (295 ft) and is the giant of the family, growing to 24 mm ($^{15}/_{16}$ in).

Satomi's pygmy seahorse (*H. satomiae*), with its local distribution around Borneo and Indonesia, is probably the world's smallest at no more than 14 mm ($^9/_{16}$ in). A pair of these little fish could sit comfortably on one key of a computer keyboard. In a world where we are obsessed with miniaturizing everything, Nature once more has the jump-start on us at every turn.

All syngnathids have a remarkable and bizarre life cycle. Seahorses are actually a group of pipefish, snake-like fish which live around most of the world's temperate and tropical oceans and have tubular mouths and long, armoured bodies. They have prehensile tails, gripping on to plants and corals to avoid being swept away by underwater currents to make up for their weakness as swimmers. And they don't have to go anywhere, as those currents sweep tiny food particles through the branches and stems of their homes. It's a commensal relationship (which means although the fish benefits, the coral comes to no harm).

Seahorses are monogamous and pairs live closely together on their own small patch of a fan coral or seagrass; it's probably just as hard for them to find each other as it is for us to find them. An arrangement that suits, as there is always plenty of room when you are this small.

They are much easier to spot close up.

Birth fathers

Even more well known is a seahorse's unique adaptation among fish: it is the males that give birth. The boys are able to have babies, as they possess a specially adapted brood pouch on their undersides.

The males keep their sperm in these pouches so all they require to get pregnant is for a female to take careful aim and drop her eggs into his open pouch, where they are fertilized and then begin to gestate.

The males keep their sperm in these pouches so all they require to get pregnant is for a female to take careful aim and drop her eggs into his open pouch, where they are fertilized and then begin to gestate. The brood pouch expands and grows over time to accommodate the developing young. Depending on the species, after 10–25 days, the male uses a set of tiny muscles to squeeze his pouch and gently squirt the perfect miniature seahorses out into the ocean; as many as 2,000 baby seahorses can be hatched from one brood. The young are precocious, all of them ready to fend for themselves out there in the big bad world. And when you are this small, everything is big.

Seahorse physical evolution doesn't just involve making everything smaller – the syngnathids are masters of camouflage. Bargibant's pygmy seahorse has evolved to mimic the pink polyps of the coral forms it inhabits, and there are also yellow fan coral species with their own specific yellow pygmy seahorse forms, accordingly.

Effective disguise is important, because seahorses have sacrificed a lot of advantages to hide among their surroundings. They are not fast swimmers and are not toxic or dangerous; they simply disappear into their background almost invisibly and secret themselves around the nooks and crannies of the coral. It seems very likely that there are more astonishing members of this unique group to be discovered – but it will be a sharp-eyed biologist or diver who finds the next!

09

CANDIRU

{Vandellia sanguinea}

A.K.A.

Cañero, toothpick fish, vampire fish

SIZE

Up to 18 cm (7 in)

HABITAT

Remote rivers

DISTINGUISHING FEATURES

Nearly transparent, turning pink after feeding

PERSONALITY

Vampire

LIKES

Blood

SPECIAL SKILLS

Gripping tightly to its victim

CONSERVATION STATUS

Insufficient data

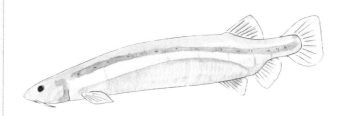

I F THERE IS one fish featured in this book that I strongly recommend you do not set out to find, it's the candiru, cañero or toothpick fish. It also goes by another name: vampire fish. And if that name doesn't scare you off, then the fact that this is the fish with the reputation for being able to swim up the urethra into the penis or vagina if you are urinating in a river, should.

The good news is that it is only found in remote and pretty inaccessible river systems in South America – particularly the Orinoco and Amazon basins. Despite the widely repeated myth, it doesn't really swim into anyone's private parts – certainly not by design. Candiru do not wait in hiding for you to arrive at the riverbank, bursting to go to the toilet. I know this first hand, having swum in such rivers where they live; of course, I went in with the all the irrational fear of meeting one, but I quickly got over it, and the need to cool down and wash far outweighed my initial concerns.

It is only found in remote and pretty inaccessible river systems in South America.

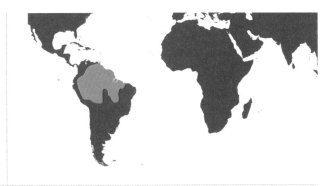

Meet the mini monster

Candiru is a member of a small elite clan of very distinct creatures that are both parasites and vampires. The definition of a parasite is an organism that makes its living off another organism, at the expense of that organism; in other words, it has a negative impact on its host's fitness (fitness meaning the success or health of the individual they exploit). This is done usually by getting free or easy food from a host or even getting the host to raise its young. While we may tend to think of parasites as worms or ticks, parasitic fish do not come so readily to mind – particularly if they are also vampires.

The traditional vampire feasts on a host's blood – once more, a very unusual habit or lifestyle among vertebrates. It is well known that two species of bat do this, but there is also a vampire finch on the Galápagos Islands, beloved of Charles Darwin himself, which is a blood drinker. Blood is nutritious but very difficult to get to, as most hosts are keen on keeping what is inside them, well, inside. It's also a very rich fluid and needs a very precise digestive system to extract the goodness from all that iron and protein. Which is exactly how the candiru has evolved – to be able to survive on nothing but blood.

For a regular and reliable supply of blood, the candiru must find a much bigger fish to attach itself to and feed on. Fortunately, the South American waterways are full of them: such as the tambaqui, red-tailed catfish or arapaima (see pages 98–101), to name but a few.

Once a suitable host is located, the candiru head for the accessible weak spot: the gills, found on the sides of the head of every species of fish. The thick gill filaments are arranged in an array of patterns that are mostly deep red in colour, indicating the large amounts of blood found in each filament. This is where the oxygen-rich water rushes over, allowing the oxygen to be absorbed from the water into the fish's gills and its body, allowing it to 'breathe' underwater.

Devious Dracula

Most gills are protected by a scale-covered flap called the operculum; gills are highly sensitive and at risk of exposure so it is essential to keep them safe and free from injury or infection – its like wearing our lungs on the outside. However, gills need to be open for water to continuously flow in and out, and that is what makes them vulnerable to small parasitic fish such as the candiru. The vampire fish sneaks up behind the larger species' head and then eases in under the operculum and into the gills.

Once inside, it uses the special tools that have given it one of its other names: the toothpick catfish. On either side of its head, it has two very small but sharp barbs that look like whiskers. These barbs are erected

Once a suitable host is located, the candiru head for an accessible weak spot: the gills.

and penetrate the victims soft gills, holding the fish in place like a grappling hook. As you'd expect the gills start to bleed from the holes made by these barbs. Which is the plan, as rather than actively suck out the blood, the natural pumping of its victim's circulatory system is enough for blood to seep into the candiru's mouth.

Once inside, it uses the special tools that have given it one of its other names: the toothpick catfish. On either side of its head, it has two very small but sharp barbs that look like whiskers. These barbs are erected and penetrate the victims soft gills, holding the fish in place like a grappling hook. As you'd expect the gills start to bleed from the holes made by these barbs. Which is the plan, as rather than actively suck out the blood, the natural pumping of its victim's circulatory system is enough for blood to seep into the candiru's mouth.

Scratching the itch

Unfortunately, the damage done to the host can sometimes be fatal if the gills are too damaged, though this is fairly unusual. The majority of the victims survive, heal and perhaps become slightly warier if they detect a little itch on the side of their heads. Many catfish species, if they have been previous victims, are very aware of the danger and will close their operculum tightly, swiping furiously with their large pectoral fins if they detect a candiru in the area. However, in a river system packed with large and lazy fish, there are plenty of innocents out there for the candiru to indulge itself.

A candiru feeding, much to the surprise of its host.

One of the most 'over-told' stories about the candiru is that it homes in on its victims by detecting and following the ammonia from urine, focusing on the source and swimming up the urethras of potential mammalian hosts; once in place, it is impossible to remove without surgery. According to some, this is a well-documented traveller's tale; however, to other sources, it's a macabre urban legend with little evidence to support it. But, either way, they are more than capable of commiting this act, they are designed for it and it certainly seems too good a story for any self-effacing candiru to want to outlive.

10

THREE-SPINED STICKLEBACK

{*Gasterosteus aculeatus*}

A.K.A.

Already has the best name

SIZE

3–4 cm (1¼–1½ in)

HABITAT

Coastal waters or freshwater lakes

DISTINGUISHING FEATURES

Three spines along its back

PERSONALITY

Defiant

LIKES

Plankton and vegetation

SPECIAL SKILLS

Nest building

CONSERVATION STATUS

Least Concern

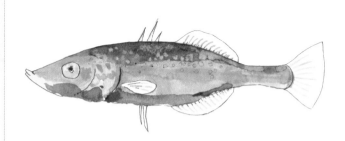

Is 'STICKLEBACK' THE best name ever bestowed on an animal? Three spines are standard but there is a 'deluxe' version with nine and even a species within the same genus that has ten. Sticklebacks are small, mostly thumb-sized freshwater fish, quite closely related to pipefish and seahorses. They are common in British, North American and European waters above latitudes of thirty degrees, and have a fascinating lifestyle. They are one of the only fish that can say they helped win a Nobel Prize.

The ancestor of the stickleback was originally marine. That changed when they became landlocked during the last Ice Age, 20,000 years ago. There are still a few relict forms that live in shallow seas, but most stickleback species live in freshwater now, and although they are fairly common and well known, few people are aware of how intense their lives can be.

Very flexible fish

One thing is clear: they are an adaptable little creature, as demonstrated by the complete decimation of sticklebacks in an Alaskan lake in North America in 1982. In a brainless attempt to make the Loberg Lake more suitable for commercially introduced trout and salmon, some bright spark released the chemical rotenone – which destroyed the lake's resident fish population almost overnight, including of course the healthy population of freshwater three-spined sticklebacks that called it home. However, as I have said, sticklebacks are adaptable, and twelve years later the population was back. How? Well, that's because some sticklebacks are anadromous (migrating from sea to freshwater like their ancestors). And it was these guys that re-found the now clear and habitable lake and settled down once more to becoming freshwater. The telltale sign of this comeback was that they retained the extra side plates of their marine form, indicating exactly where they had come from.

Despite being able to live in either fresh or saltwater, sticklebacks need certain types of vegetation to feed in and complete their life cycle. Sticklebacks are unusual in being nest-building fish and need the correct materials to construct these essential breeding structures. The male stickleback is the actual builder of this piscean edifice, which is certainly an elaborate and meticulously constructed affair. Firstly, a small pit or depression is dug into the silt of the sea or lakebed. The next task is to collect materials for the walls, which mostly consist of small pieces of vegetation or algae. The males dart in and out, gathering

Female sticklebacks are approached by males using bizarre zigzag dances.

water weeds and loose vegetation to bring back to the depression they have just made. The materials are then glued together using a unique substance known as 'spiggin', which is only produced by stickleback kidneys. This glycoprotein glue sticks the vegetation together to form a sort of bower. The fish then dive through the bower several times to create a tunnel in which the eggs will be laid.

Once completed, this construction becomes the centre of each stickleback's universe; now all that's left to do is to entice a female stickleback into the castle to mate. The male approaches the female using a bizarre zigzag dance, before poking his head into the nest as if to indicate that she should place her eggs precisely there. If this heavy hint is taken, that's exactly what she does; the sticky eggs are laid on the bower's vegetative stems, and then the male fertilizes them. He then chases her away in a rather ungentlemanly fashion, as raising the brood is his role, and his alone.

Females see red

Females won't just lay eggs in any male's nest, as they don't want to risk childcare on a slob or a fool. The only way to assess the quality of the males is visually and this is done by looking at the intensity of the red colouration on his underparts. When they are ready to breed, male sticklebacks change colour dramatically. Their eyes turn a wonderful iridescent blue, while their throats and bellies turn a very bright red. And the more intense the red, the stronger and fitter the male is – and so the females are drawn to the brightest red male in town.

Male sticklebacks change colour strikingly when they are ready to breed.

Males are also triggered by red but in a very different way. From their point of view, this red colour is like a rag to a bull (in fact, bulls are blue-green colour blind and can't see the colour red at all). Male sticklebacks react immediately to this visual stimulus and go on the attack. So much so, that one stickleback, kept in a domestic

Although most
have three
spines, some
have two and
some have four.

fish tank on a windowsill, was observed to rush to the defence of his nest every morning when he saw the red post van pull up outside. This home happened to belong to the biologist Niko Tinbergen who, along with Konrad Lorenz, is seen as the father of ethology – the study of animal behaviour – and went on to win a Nobel Prize for his work with sticklebacks, among other creatures.

The garish red colour that so excites the instincts of sticklebacks is generated by pigments absorbed from their food. It is at least superficially clear, then, that the redder the male, the better he is likely to be at feeding himself – indicating his superiority as a father. And in reverse, males that are sick or diseased appear less red, indicating an inability to provide for his offspring.

Another one of Tinbergen's discoveries was made when he placed a mirror in front of a fired-up red-bellied male. The raging fish confronted it like a rival, but after becoming confused by the exact matching movements and colour of his 'rival', he eventually wandered away to rearrange his nest or eat something. Tinbergen called this 'displacement behaviour' – when the fish is confronted with an impossible dilemma, it loses interest and its attention is turned to something more trivial – perhaps something we can all identify with at times.

SPOTTED LANTERNFISH

{Myctophum punctatum}

THE DIMINUTIVE LANTERNFISH may look like Minions, but they are probably the most numerous vertebrate on planet Earth. Even so, few of us have ever heard of them, largely because most of them live at depths attainable only by the hardiest and strongest of submersibles (approximately 1,220 m / 4,000 ft). So, if that is the case, how do we know there are so many of them?

On the radar

The first clue to the abyssal ubiquity of lanternfish emerged when ichthyologists attempted to see how deep the ocean was by using sonar. This is the use of sound waves that are emitted and then recorded when they bounce back; the length of time the echo takes to return allows distances and shapes to be judged

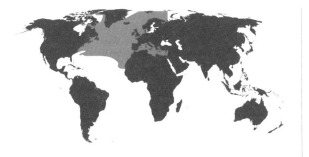

Lanternfish could account for as much as 65 per cent of the fish biomass in the deep sea.

very accurately and was a trick bats evolved to have millions of years ago. The scientists were a little surprised when the sonar signals bounced back much quicker than had been predicted, indicating an unlikely shallowness in the deepest parts of the ocean. But after further investigations, they realized that the sonar readings were not originating from the seabed at all – but rather a huge and dense shoal of lanternfish so vast that it made their measuring equipment respond as if it was the bottom of the ocean. It's almost as if a flock of birds was so enormous that radar registered them as the sky!

It has been estimated since that lanternfish could account for as much as 65 per cent of the fish biomass in the deep sea. Technically, the deep sea is everything below the reach of sunlight, which is about 1,000 m (3,280 ft) down. This area accounts for 95 per cent of the entire liveable habitat on the planet and lanternfish are the most numerous animals in that space. In conclusion, there really is an unfathomable number of lanternfish in the oceans.

Lanternfish like the darkness and of course every twelve hours or so, when night falls, the whole sea becomes dark and then they do something strange. Every night the lanternfish embark on a vertical migration en masse, travelling up and down rather than north to south. This daily pattern is driven by the mobility of their food supply. Lanternfish subsist on zooplankton – the myriad microscopic larvae of crabs, lobsters, anemones, fish, worms, jellyfish and the many other submarine animals that form a rich bouillabaisse in seawater. These innumerable tiny creatures also move from the depths together into the shallows every night – and the lanternfish that love eating this floating menagerie follow them up. This journey is a perilous one, as they enter a danger zone where they can easily fall prey to squid and the other grotesque fish species. Some of these predators will also follow the shoals up towards the surface at night, but it is still safer than during the day when this region of the sea is full of penguins, seals, dolphins, sharks and other daytime predators. Essentially lanternfish live in a giant perpetual game of aquatic hide and seek to avoid getting eaten.

Turning on the lights

Lanternfish also have another trick to keep out of danger – and this trick is the source of their intriguing name. Like many other creatures of the abyssal deep, lanternfish can produce their own light. Called bioluminescence, we are discovering this ability to create their own light is present in an ever-growing number of animals – from glow-worms to bobtail squid; however, this trait is at its most diverse in deep-sea fish species.

Explained simply, bioluminescence works by combining a naturally occurring protein called luciferin with an enzyme called luciferase; they react together, sometimes with other biochemicals that vary between species, ultimately producing light in different shades of blue, red and even yellow. Every chemical reaction produces some form of energy, so I guess it should be no surprise that, along with sound or heat, a simple reaction can produce light. Most species of lanternfish have light-emitting organs called photophores, which contain all the chemicals in readiness for use. The arrangement of these photophores vary from species to species and can be found in most parts of their bodies, whether up near their eyes, along their underparts or in many other places; many have recognizable patterns to aid identification in the dark by fish-watchers in bathyspheres.

The true purpose of these spectral lights is not completely known.

Glowing in the dark

The true purpose of these spectral lights is not completely known. One of the latest theories suggests that these lights disrupt their outlines when seen from underneath, creating a sort of negative camouflage in the dark, and thus a defence against predators. In some species of lanternfish, the males and females have photophores in different parts of their bodies, perhaps indicating that the lights might have something more to do with sexual selection. These mysteries might be more quickly solved if the fish did not live in the most inaccessible zone of the Earth's biosphere. They are so difficult to study in their natural habitat (and it is even harder to create that habitat in ours) that it is highly likely that this speculation will continue for some time. Perhaps some species' lights can be flashed in a sort of 'Morse code' for the fish to signal one another in the darkness, like an ancient social network. Maybe some lights can be used as torches in the dark, though the light produced is usually too weak to see how this would work. Like many deep-ocean fish, lanternfish have very large eyes, and I think there is something wonderful about the idea that these fishy minions are swimming around slowly, using their face torches to make sure they are going the right way or to tell spooky deep-sea stories at camp.

Lights on the underside of the body break up the fish's silhouette when viewed from below, perhaps making them harder to see by predators

12

LEOPARD MORAY EEL

{Enchelycore pardalis}

A.K.A.

Dragon moray,
Hawaiian dragon

SIZE

Up to 92 cm (3 ft)

HABITAT

Mainly warm water
reefs

**DISTINGUISHING
FEATURES**

Multicoloured, double
set of jaws

PERSONALITY

Secretive

LIKES

Hunting with groupers

SPECIAL SKILLS

Forms slimy mucus on
its skin

**CONSERVATION
STATUS**

Least Concern

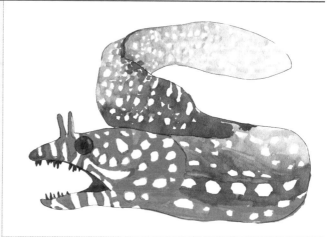

M Y DEPICTIONS OF fish might not always be entirely anatomically precise, but they should be good enough to serve as an introduction to the real thing. In this case, you might well think that I have gone too far and taken liberties. However, the leopard or dragon moray eel really is as colourful as I have depicted.

Moray eels are a large family comprised of about 200 mostly marine species found in all areas of the tropical and temperate oceans where light can penetrate. There are a few freshwater species and a few more in polar waters, while others have a somewhat dull colouration; I chose the leopard moray eel because of the prevalence of the colour purple – it's not often a fish illustrator gets to use this colour.

Malevolent morays

Morays are predominantly warm-water, predatory reef fish. They have evolved long, sinuous bodies for flowing movements to perfectly fit in the crevices found among the coral and rocks of ocean reefs; they almost appear to 'pour' rather than swim, a smooth movement that is hypnotic, if not a little malevolent. They also possess a great sense of smell; those 'horns' on the leopard moray eel pictured are actually elongated nostril tubes allowing them to detect the scent of prey.

Anyone who has watched any of the *Alien* movies will be very familiar with the idea of a predatory animal having a small mouth contained within a larger set of jaws. Morays also have both inner and outer jaws with teeth. They hunt in small confined spaces and have evolved to grab the more elusive prey items with thin sharp teeth, while the inner jaws, which resemble a pair of long-nosed pliers, also hold it so it doesn't escape. They can grab prey that is much larger than you would think possible. Like snakes, morays then gradually 'walk' their prey into the cavernous tube that is their stomach by incrementally squeezing it along with their muscles. Unlike snakes, however, morays can't dislocate their front jaws but use those back or pharyngeal jaws (which are naturally present in all 30,000 or so species of teleosts or bony fish) to slowly swallow their food. This snatch-and-grab technique is highly effective and unlike the majority of bony fish which use some form of suction to get food into their mouths, like water-borne vacuum cleaners. So effective is it that morays are often the apex predators (that is, the predator at the top of the food chain) in many reef habitats.

In 2006, a marine biologist named Redouan Bshary was studying the behaviour of cleaner fish in the Red Sea, when he witnessed a

The snatch-and-grab technique of morays is highly effective.

These eels vary in colour and pattern, but all have those fearsome needle-sharp teeth.

spotted coral grouper, another top predator in that habitat, swim up to a giant moray eel that was poking its head out of its daytime nook. He thought he was about to witness a scrap between the two bullies of the reef but instead witnessed something new and utterly remarkable. The grouper shook its head at the moray, which emerged from its burrow and joined the grouper as they swam off together.

These actions were observed repeatedly over time and it emerged that the groupers were enlisting the help of the morays when hunting, even leading the eels to where they had lost a prey fish that had escaped into a reef crevice. The moray would then wriggle inside and either catch the food for itself or force the fish to swim out again – in which case the grouper would be able to grab it. The technical term for this behaviour is 'interspecific communicative and coordinated hunting'. It's extremely rare in nature and no one knows how long they have been doing it!

Superspines

Morays have an unusually large number of vertebrae. Humans and other mammals – even giraffes – have thirty-three, but it is not uncommon for a moray eel to have more than a hundred of these small interlocking bones. Other moray species such as the metre-long ribbon eel (*Rhinomuraena quaesita*), which is a lurid blue and green colour, have as many as 258 vertebrae.

Another intriguing moray trait is that their skin is covered in a layer of slimy mucus, which allows them to avoid injury from the sharp edges of their coral and rock homes; the skin is also laced with a distasteful toxin. This substance deters other fish from preying on them, although some sharks and groupers do indulge on occasion. Ironically, this slime is almost unnecessary as moray eel flesh is almost unpalatable, and not fit for human consumption. This is because, in their internal organs, they harbour a toxin known as ciguatera. Though completely harmless to its host, this poison is produced by a dinoflagellate micro-organism that commonly lives inside some marine fish – if a human ingests this toxin, it usually results in symptoms such as diarrhoea, vomiting, drowsiness, heart arrhythmia and even death.

Creatures of the night

The family have some very cool names that all reflect their amazing patterns, such as the snowflake or the geometric eel, but despite their prolific and complex patterns and colours, many moray eel species are actually nocturnal. The patterning is likely disruptive camouflage among all the colourful life on the reef.

Leave well alone, even if you're stranded on a deserted atoll!

To the human eye, morays have a sinister or vicious appearance, as they are often seen with their heads poking out of a dark, underwater cranny, their mouths wide open to show off their needle-sharp teeth, looking like they are sizing you up as a meal. However, this not threatening behaviour – morays have such small gills that they need to do this in order to aid breathing. Even so, you would do well to keep at arm's length from moray eels on a dive; they can be very territorial and can be highly aggressive when disturbed. They have even been known to react to their own reflection in face masks.

GUPPY

{Poecilia reticulata}

13

A.K.A.

Millionfish,
rainbowfish

SIZE

Males: up to 3.5 cm
(1½ in)
Females: up to 6 cm
(2½ in)

HABITAT

Almost anywhere

DISTINGUISHING FEATURES

A range of different
colours

PERSONALITY

Tough and adaptable

LIKES

Strength in numbers

SPECIAL SKILLS

Birth control

CONSERVATION STATUS

Least Concern

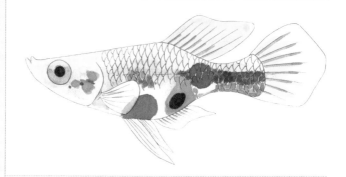

A NYONE WHO HAS kept aquarium fish will, at some point, more than likely have encountered a guppy. It is one of the most colourful and surprisingly robust fish on the planet, and yet no bigger than a postage stamp. Even so, the biology of the guppy is as intriguing and colourful as the tails the males of the species wave around to get attention.

Originally, guppies derived from the Caribbean, although the first one to be scientifically described was named as long ago as 1859 from a specimen caught in Venezuela. Another was described from a specimen caught in Trinidad in 1866, and given the name *Girardinus guppii* after the rather dashing British naturalist that had collected it – Robert John Lechmere Guppy. As this was the first name officially given, the original scientific name stuck and the fish's English name rapidly caught on as 'guppy'.

Guppies can survive and thrive in almost any situation.

Flamboyant but friendly

Guppies have several agreeable facets to their nature that have made them very popular around the world, as well as numerous. The first thing you might notice about a guppy is the amazing colours of the males and their flamboyant, over-sized tails and fins. Females are somewhat larger – sometimes half as big again as the males – and lack any of the ostentatious extensions and embellishments with which the males are adorned. Despite their plainer appearance, females are very much in charge in the world of the guppy.

Guppies have very adaptable eating habits, devouring whatever edible prey is most common where they are living, whether that be algae or insect larvae. This lack of epicurean and relatively minimal appetites is one the keys to their success (though they do occasionally eat each other), but there are many more.

Guppies also have the life skills that mean they can survive and thrive in almost any situation in which they find themselves. One of their major adaptations is viviparity – that is, the bearing of live young. The females give birth to tiny little guppies after a gestation period of 21–30 days – about as long as most songbird species – and a lone female can give birth to as many as 200 miniatures of herself over six hours (though this figure is more usually around 30–60). Females are sexually mature at ten weeks old, live to about two years (being fertile throughout) and can produce two or three generations every year. This means that a single female guppy can push out up to 1,200 babies in her lifetime. Admittedly, some other fish species can produce eggs in their millions, but there are other traits of guppies that give them a reproductive and survival edge.

Outside influence

Guppy behaviour varies according to environmental influences. If they live in water where there are lots of predators, they tend to live longer, form larger shoals and become more fertile. These traits counteract the impact of any predation and maintain a high and healthy guppy population. However, if there are few or no predators, the guppies present manage their population according to how much food and space there is. They will also shoal less and become less fertile, thus reducing the breeding potential of each individual, as the likelihood of losing lots of the population is low. If a predator is introduced, they will then revert to flooding the habitat with lots of baby guppies in order to increase the possibility of survival. In essence, guppies control their populations according to circumstances.

After the aquarium trade boomed, more and more flamboyant guppy variants began to appear.

Despite the productivity of guppies, they are very precise and careful with their breeding behaviour. Many fish haphazardly eject millions of eggs as the males fertilize them externally, spraying milt in the general direction of the eggs; it's a hit-and-miss method, but it works for the majority of fish species. Guppies, on the other hand, fertilize their eggs internally. The male has a gonopodium hidden away in his anal fin, which is a kind of tube in which it keeps sacks of sperm. When he mates with a female, the tube is pushed into the female's vent and the sperm is released; this technique reduces waste and lowers the risk of not fertilizing the eggs, similar to mammals. This method is also further refined: once the female has received the sperm, she can now control its use, storing it for up to eight months. In the unlikely but chilling event that all the males are killed or eaten, then the female will still be able to reproduce months later and even be solely responsible for repopulating the waters where she lives. Another female trait is polyandry – the ability or inclination to mate with more than one male. This also means that a female can store more than one male's sperm at a time, enabling her to produce young long after the males have disappeared. This ability to give birth to young fertilized by different males also means that they can even keep their genetics healthily varied and viable.

Tiny but tough

The innate ability to survive against all odds does have a downside in this modern age. When humans decided to introduce guppies to many different habitats around the world, erroneously believing the fish would help to decimate disease-rich mosquito populations by feasting on their larvae, all they did was unleash a tiny army. This platoon of aquarium fish was effectively prepared to take over much of the world to the detriment of other fish and ecosystems. Guppies now threaten biodiversity in countries as far away as Trinidad, Pakistan and Cambodia and are very difficult, if not impossible, to remove.

Once the female has received the sperm, she can store it for up to eight months.

All these intricate and intriguing details of the guppy's life are so well-known because the guppy is extremely robust and resilient, making it one of the most studied animals on the planet. It can now be found in almost every laboratory and biological establishment around the world. Even though its life secrets are somewhat laid bare, this doesn't stop it from remaining beguiling and appealing.

So, the next time you pass by a fish tank and see a cute and colourful little fish performing a fancy dance next to another, surrounded by lots of little replicas of themselves, don't be fooled; if you give a guppy an inch, it will take a mile – it is programmed to take over the world in any way it can.

14

BROWNBANDED BAMBOO SHARK

{Chiloscyllium punctatum}

A.K.A.

Carpet shark, cat shark, walking shark

SIZE

Up to 1 m (3 ft 3 in)

HABITAT

Coral reefs and tide pools

DISTINGUISHING FEATURES

Bold stripes and whisker-like barbels

PERSONALITY

Nocturnal

LIKES

Shrimp, scallop, squid and small fish

SPECIAL SKILLS

Survival out of water

CONSERVATION STATUS

Near Threatened

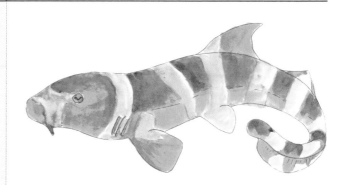

WHILE THEY ARE larger than all the other fish in this section, the reason I have included brownbanded bamboo sharks is that, at no more than 1 m (3 ft 3 in) in length when fully grown, it can be considered a small shark. It's also one of the most beautiful sharks out there, with its dazzling banding. It's somewhat of a shame that those bold stripes begin to fade with age and they end up looking a little drab. Accordingly, my illustration is of a youngster. However, what makes these diminutive sharks worthy of an appearance among my choice of fifty fish is that you can sometimes find these fish on land.

Bamboo sharks (also known as carpet sharks) aren't scared of being out of water. They are, in fact, able to live for up to twelve hours out of the water with seemingly no ill effect. And the reason they have developed this super-skill is because they live in the intertidal zone – the area of the coast where depths can quickly vary from several feet deep to bone dry within a very short period. As tides work over an approximate twelve-hour cycle, this is the length of time that most stranded sharks would be exposed, and it would certainly pay off evolutionarily to be resistant to drying out and suffocating within that period. The pay-off for such extreme behaviour is decent, in that this ability enables bamboo sharks to prowl the tidal pools exposed by the falling tide. Such temporary reservoirs will often contain edibles such as crabs, fish or shrimp left stranded with no chance of escape until the tide comes back to re-immerse them. These are food resources that few aquatic animals can access, though there is some competition from seabirds and scavenging mammals.

Not coming up for air

They can live out of water for so long because they can reduce the amount of oxygen they need. They do this by slowing their heart rate and breathing and by reducing the blood flow to their bodies and even certain parts of their brains. This ability is known as hypoxia (and is similar to how human physiology behaves at high altitudes) – essentially, bamboo sharks don't suffocate out of water. This is a survival strategy comparable with few other fish, because not only are the sharks largely unopposed when foraging for food but they remain out of reach of bigger predators while doing so.

Bamboo sharks are able to live for up to twelve hours out of the water.

Add to this their tendency to perform their stealth hunting at night, and the behaviour becomes successfully secretive and sly. Their strange, slit-like eyes and whisker-like organs or barbels (very similar to a catfish's) has led them to be alternatively known as 'cat sharks' (though the true catsharks – family Scyliorhinidae – are a more distantly related group). Their intermediate habitat between shoreline and reef is ideally adjacent to a muddy or sandy bottom, as bamboo sharks like to wallow down into the silt and remain invisible during the day. They emerge at night and, using the very sensitive barbels to feel their way around in the soft mud or around the surface and fissures of the reef, hunt for small crustaceans. When they find themselves prowling the tide pools, they try to eat most things they happen upon, using their small yet powerful jaws like nutcrackers to crush any meals that come packaged in hard shells.

Bamboo sharks try to eat most things they happen upon.

Small but perfect

Bamboo sharks are mostly found in the Western Indo-Pacific, ranging from Japan down to Australia, and are fairly common in their core distribution. They may be more numerous than we think, owing to their secretive habits, and we maybe underestimating how many there are. However, bamboo sharks are also in demand, as these small and quite beautiful sharks are a favourite of the pet trade. Aquarists love them, and in many respects, they are the perfect piscean pet, as they don't take up much room, are relatively robust and live for up to twenty years. They also have the capability of laying plenty of eggs in captivity and are pretty easy to breed. Baby bamboo sharks hatch out of eggs laid by the females and left on the sea floor on or around the coral reef. In common with other cartilaginous fish, their eggs are flattened, edged and have filaments on each of their four corners, and resemble alien seed pods. Each contains a perfect little shark, but the hatched pods can also be found desiccated on the shore, along with the many other egg pods of skates, rays and sharks. The widespread destruction of coral reefs is, of course, having a huge impact on bamboo shark populations, adding further damage to that done by the illegal aquarium trade, which is the most dangerous threat to this species.

Bamboo sharks are eaten in South-east Asia and considered a delicacy in Australia, but they are not very easy to catch; they have flattened tails that curve and curl around things to make the sharks hard to detach from rocks and branches, though the tails are not fully prehensile. This versatility of movement, along with their terrestrial habits, has given them an alternative name of 'walking sharks'. They have wide and powerful pectoral fins (the appendages closest to the head and almost on the underside) and look as if they are walking along the seabed when submerged. A close cousin, the long-tailed epaulette shark, has taken this ability a stage further and will emerge from the water and walk across land to get to another tide pool when foraging, and generally gets there relatively unscathed.

While the idea that sharks can walk across land might be somewhat disconcerting to many, brownbanded bamboo sharks are harmless. And the old adage is true: they have more to fear from us than we ever do from them.

That disruptive colour pattern works well to camouflage them against their natural backdrop.

15

RED-BELLIED PIRANHA

{*Pygocentrus nattereri*}

A.K.A.

Red piranha, caribe, piraya

SIZE

Up to 60 cm (2 ft)

HABITAT

Freshwater rivers

DISTINGUISHING FEATURES

Strong jaws and razor-sharp teeth

PERSONALITY

Bitey

LIKES

Meat

SPECIAL SKILLS

Communication

CONSERVATION STATUS

Not evaluated

THIS SOUTH AMERICAN carnivore is the well-known, small, bloodthirsty fish featured in James Bond and horror films. Not all Piranhas are actually that small, larger examples would easily cover a dinner plate, but their infamy mostly hangs on their habits and what they keep in their mouths.

Piranha have incredible teeth which take the form of perfect serrated triangles of dentine that fit together inside their mouths like a jigsaw in a perfect arc of vicious weaponry. They can bite both very quickly and with inordinate power: the pressure has been recently studied by ichthyologists and is, pound for pound, more powerful than a great white shark. Although how they have evolved such an overpowered bite for such a relatively small fish has nothing to do with trying to compete with sharks.

Piranhas are members of a large family – the Serrasalmidae (from the Latin for 'serrated salmon', as you may have suspected). There are ninety species inhabiting the Atlantic side of South America below the Andes, with successful introductions to a few other areas. Their body size ranges from a coin to the metre-long monsters known as pacu, which have their own unique set of teeth that look more like a cow's than a fish's, and that's because they eat nuts. And it's this fact that explains the evolution of the piranhas massive bite. The ancestors of the red-bellied piranha were nut 'crackers', turning to meat for subsistence once their a formidable bite had evolved.

The fish of nightmares

The popular legend of the viciousness of piranha originated from an American president: Theodore Roosevelt. He travelled to Brazil on one of his well-known wild excursions (often referred to as naturalist expeditions but usually for shooting). On one occasion, he was given a set of educational demonstrations by locals: one being that of a snake eating another snake and another involving a cow. To show the dangers of the native Amazonian fishes, locals pushed a cow into the water; the water soon appeared to be boiling as the cow disappeared into a cloud of blood and muddy water, and within minutes all that was left was its skeleton. When Roosevelt returned and wrote his memoirs, the legend of the piranha was properly born.

The pressure is, pound for pound, more powerful than a great white shark.

The accuracy of the details around this story may require further scrutiny. It seems entirely possible that it is true when one regards the dental weaponry and power the fish are packing, but it was the time of year that mattered. Piranha are among the most prolific fish in South American river systems: if you put bait out, the first bite is usually a piranha – and if you are not using fishing wire trace, then the odds are that it will chew through your line and carry away all your tackle as well. Piranha can also assemble into huge shoals numbering in their thousands. This behaviour has probably more to do with defence than hunting. Perhaps surprisingly, piranha are not the top dogs in the waters they live in; they are a popular food item of caiman, giant otters and Amazon river dolphins, which all find them to be good eating and only generally succumb to the fish themselves when they are dead or dying.

Piranha teeth are like perfect little pyramids of pain.

Land of the drowning trees

The Amazon is a place of extremes: the river flows through the trees in the rainy season, but in the dry season the water drops by as much as 20 m (65 ft). Once when I was in South America, I saw a fallen tree wedged into crown branches of another tree; I asked a boat captain how that could happen and he casually told me that it had floated in – that was as high as the water gets in the rainy season. How else could a huge tree end up in another tree in the middle of the rainforest?

When the rains are falling, the fish head out among trees to search for food and to breed amid the roots and leaf litter which form the river bottom for the season. However, during the dry season, the river shrinks to a trickle of its former self, exposing sandbars, revealing steep banks and stranding broken and damaged trees. As the pools and remaining areas of water become more concentrated, most of the fish are exposed, starving and struggling for oxygen. This is not the time to start dipping your toes in – or, indeed, push a cow in.

The talking fish

Red-bellied piranha talk. When you catch one and very carefully remove the fishhook, it makes weird 'gakk gakk' sounds. This noise is created by squeezing pockets of air through their gills, and the sounds are well known in the Amazon. Recent studies suggest that they don't make just one noise but have quite a wide range of vocabulary. While indulging in a feeding frenzy in a drying pool, piranhas communicate with one another, in effect shouting at others to leave them alone and thus avoiding accidentally being turned into a meal themselves. This remarkable discovery has revealed a whole new level of understanding of fish communication of which we were, until recently, completely ignorant (see the clownfish, pages 72–5).

They don't make just one noise but have quite a wide range of vocabulary.

As scary and voracious as they are, piranhas themselves are ironically good eating. They are so common and easy to catch that piranha stew is a common meal in South America. The favourite cooking technique is fairly simple: drop large chunks of piranha, including the head and tail, into a big pot and cook them with onions and spices. It can be one of the stranger things to eat, particularly when you move your spoon and a saw-toothed skull breaks the surface of the soup!

It may happen, one day, that you have to pick a piranha up out of the water, as unlikely as that may seem. Even if you get hold of their dorsal fin, you will need to be aware of another nasty side of the piranha: they possess a small spine on their dorsal fin which can deliver a nasty stab – and this is very likely to happen as you will be so focused on avoiding their snapping teeth as they wriggle and writhe; the last thing you want is to lose your grip and get a nasty nip, trust me.

16

ORANGE
CLOWNFISH

{Amphiprion percula}

A.K.A.

Percula clownfish,
clown anemonefish

SIZE

Around 8 cm (3 in)

HABITAT

In and around
anemones

**DISTINGUISHING
FEATURES**

Orange with three
white stripes

PERSONALITY

Fastidious

LIKES

A tidy anemone

SPECIAL SKILLS

Changing sex

**CONSERVATION
STATUS**

Least Concern

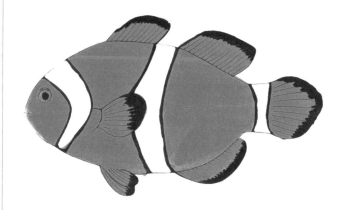

THERE ARE THIRTY species of clownfish in the world and not all of them look like the famous cartoon character, Nemo, though several do. Clownfish are found in the warm waters of the Indo-Pacific, including the Red Sea. They are always associated with coral reefs and almost always associated with hiding in the tentacles of sea anemones. However, this symbiotic relationship is much more complicated than it looks.

Sea anemones are venomous and deliver their sting via their arms. If you accidentally brush against one, thousands of tiny stinging cells called cnidocytes (also present in many jellyfish) burst into life – and you! Each cnidocyte has capsules with harpoons coiled up inside of them, all of which are poised in perpetual readiness. Brushing against a tentacle causes many of these

Not all clownfish look like the famous cartoon character, Nemo, though several do.

capsules to burst, and they fire out their harpoons. Each harpoon is loaded with a dose of venom, which it injects into its attacker or potential food item, whether accidental or not. These actions are performed on a scale far too small for us to see with the naked eye but are dramatic when observed under the microscope. What might look like a rash on human skin is really lots of tiny wounds caused by the impact of thousands of little harpoons fired into your skin.

Sting dodgers

Most sea anemones are harmless to us, as their toxins are designed to stun and kill fish rather than people; however, there are a couple of anemone species that are worth avoiding. One of them is the amazingly named hell's fire anemone from the family of night anemones, which is only found in Japan. There are also a couple of species in the family Stichodactylidae in the Indo-Pacific that should be avoided. Even so, it is this family of anemones that is most often found to be housing clownfish. This, of course, begs the question of how these small, entirely edible, anemone-sized fish can survive where angelfish fear to swim.

The relationship between the two creatures (sea anemones are animals rather than plants, despite their name) is unusual, complicated and pretty special in the animal kingdom. Perhaps the most obvious benefit is for the fish – they get to hide inside a deadly predator trap that prevents them from being eaten. Clownfish never stray too far from their host, laying their eggs, raising their young, sleeping and generally living their lives in, around and on the anemone. The anemone gets direct benefits from the food and excrement dropped by its messy house guests, which provide all the nutrients it needs – the true definition of a symbiotic relationship, where one species can't live without the other.

There is an unproven idea that having a colourful fish frolicking around in a waving tentacle garden might lure other fish in for a meal – but there is another benefit the anemone gets from this relationship, which involves movement. The clownfish dive in and out of the tentacles, nipping between them and, by doing this, massage the whole anemone, leaving no area unattended. This movement gives the anemone its greatest benefit: the toing and froing helps to aerate and circulate the water around what can otherwise be a fairly a static host, keeping the anemone healthy and clean. Research has shown that an anemone with a resident clownfish grows bigger and faster than one without, thus providing a massive benefit in the ultra-competitive world of the coral reef.

Clownfish never stray too far from their host.

Stunning secrets

However, I still haven't explained how the clownfish doesn't get stung or how the anemone seems to recognize that only this one fish is its friend, rather than a foe (or, indeed, food). Although there are several different hypotheses, there is yet no definitive answer. The most current is that clownfish produce a unique mucus that covers their bodies and that the anemones' automatic attack system doesn't recognize – this enables the fish to 'ghost' in and out, almost as if they were wearing a cloak of invisibility. There are also a few other species that can hide among the tentacles of an anemone, but none of them does it so independently and seamlessly. For clownfish, life without an anemone simply does not exist. In the real world, poor *Nemo*'s journey, as depicted by the lead character in the popular animated movie which was modelled on a clownfish, simply couldn't ever happen.

Understandably, clownfish have evolved an entire life cycle around their cnidarian homes, using them to house one sometimes extended family. The largest fish in the family is the female, which dominates; underneath are the males, in a size-based hierarchy. The next largest is usually the father – the others tend to be the juvenile males, enlisted to help maintain the small colony, cleaning and diving in and out of the anemone to keep it fresh and aerated. Clownfish all have OCD and are fastidious cleaners, not just of the anemone home but often the area around it as well – well, the best house guests are always the tidiest!

Clownfish home life gets stranger, though: this size-based hierarchy all changes if, for example, the big female disappears, dies of old age or gets eaten by a cunning predator – and it would have to be cunning enough to wait for the split second when she had strayed too far from the safety of the anemone's waving arms. If the female is lost, then the next biggest fish – the dominant male – transforms and becomes a 'she', immediately taking over as the matriarch of the colony. Consequently, the next male in size takes over the role of father and all the other fish in effect move up a notch. In this way, the colony can continue despite the loss of its most important or dominant member.

The biggest clownfish is always the female.

It's no wonder this clever symbiosis evolved in a way – once clownfish move in, you can't ever get rid of them, it seems!

Chapter 3

ASTOUNDING GIANTS

Water covers around 71 per cent of our planet – and the oceans hold about 96.5 per cent of it – so it is no wonder really, with all that space, that some fish can grow to incredible sizes. None can quite match the blue whale (Balaenoptera musculus) in size (the biggest animal to ever grace our planet), but that doesn't mean that some species of fish aren't almost as impressive. There are plenty of massive fish species and many have, at some stage in our history, inspired more than their fair share of legends and sea-monster myths. While these are awe-inspiring as fiction, I hope to show that the reality is even more amazing.

17

GOLIATH TIGERFISH

{Hydrocynus goliath}

A.K.A.

Giant tigerfish, *mbenga*

SIZE

Around 1.5 m (5 ft)

HABITAT

Congo river basin

DISTINGUISHING FEATURES

Big teeth

PERSONALITY

Demonic possession

LIKES

Eating other fish

SPECIAL SKILLS

Destroying fishing equipment

CONSERVATION STATUS

Least Concern

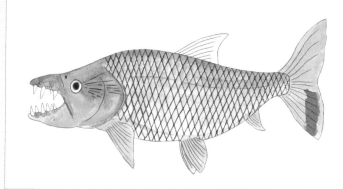

AT FIRST GLANCE, this looks like no other freshwater fish found in the rivers of the world. It is undoubtedly large at 1.5 m (4 ft 11 in) and heavy at 50 kg (110 lb) and sits in the ray-finned fish order, which includes the tetras and piranhas of this world. But its most outstanding features are, of course, those teeth. The goliath tigerfish is a fish that would not only haunt your nightmares – it can haunt you in the real world, too.

Goliath tigerfish have the same number of teeth as the average human – thirty-two – but they are not safely tucked away in an assortment of molars and canines – they are all pointed daggers that resemble those of a Nile crocodile in both size and form. They have evolved to bite into other species of large fish and tear large chunks of flesh out of them.

Congo monster

The Congo in Central and West Africa is a vast and impressive river system, perfect for hiding monsters, both mythical and real. Goliath tigerfish are also known as giant tigerfish or – locally – *mbenga*, which translates roughly as 'dangerous fish' and derives from the name of the spirit which is said to enter its body to make it so monstrous. It is most at home among the many cataracts and rapids which intersperse the length of this deep and dark waterway – what could be thought of as the most dangerous places of a very dangerous place. Mbenga wait in the eddies and slack water to take advantage of other species of fish struggling in the current or disoriented by the swirling chaos of the rapids; even the noise can be enough to confuse some lost fish. But even if you know where they live, catching one is still no easy task: as even with the biggest and most modern baited hook, their jaws are so full of their own sharp hardware that there isn't much room for anything else.

Local fishermen do not intentionally target mbenga, and not just because of the complicated and precarious places they live but more to do with the fact they have their nets shredded by those sharp teeth and the fish's ability to smash to pieces even the most high-tech fishing gear; frankly, there are easier and more tasty fish on which to concentrate. The Congo is a river jam-packed with hundreds of fish species, many very edible indeed, including vundu (*Heterobranchus longifilis* – a giant, airbreathing catfish), West African lungfish (*Protopterus annectens*) and more than eighty cichlid (Cichlidae) species. It is also home to some very big West African crocodiles – probably the only animal that is likely to take on a goliath tigerfish in these waters.

The goliath tigerfish is a fish that would haunt your nightmares.

Dogs and tigers

The species' scientific name from when it was first described in 1898 is a little confusing. *Hydrocynus* literally translates as 'water dog' which, of course, is distinctly at odds with the most widely used English name of tigerfish. However, the closely related, but much more common and considerably smaller, African tigerfish (*H. vittatus*) has a striped pattern on its tail and was already known as a 'tigerfish' before either was given its Latin binomial. The goliath tigerfish was first described in the nineteenth century by George Albert Boulenger, a Belgian-British naturalist who was well connected with West Africa when the region was known as the Belgian Congo during the dark and disgraceful times of colonialism. Boulenger was the prolific describer and namer of 1,096 fish species, 556 amphibians and 875 reptiles. It's hard to imagine that the goliath tigerfish wasn't one of the most exciting of his career.

Despite its toughness in other departments such as dentition and musculature, tigerfish are sensitive souls. They are predominantly found in warm, fast-flowing and oxygen-rich freshwater and struggle in anything approaching less than optimum conditions, making the presence of the species a good indicator of the health of a river system.

Just like a croc, their teeth don't fit inside their own jaws.

As the species is overwhelmingly sedentary, sticking to their own patch in the river catchment, biologists have long pondered various hypotheses of how tigerfish have got to so many places. There are five species in its genus (along with a possible five more 'cryptic species' awaiting official description and naming). Tigerfish (*H. brevis*) inhabits the river Nile, blue tigerfish (*H. tanzaniae*) – the most recently described in 1986 – lives in Tanzanian rivers, elongate tigerfish (*H. forskahlii*) is found in much of West Africa, while the aforementioned African tigerfish is common over much of sub-Saharan Africa. Many freshwater fish species have evolved to be quite robust because of the ever-changing nature of rivers, and in the case of some catfish species they are tough enough to travel through swamps or feeder streams, or can even cross land. So the question remains: how did the vicious but very particular tigerfish manage to get to all these far and remote places?

Shifting habitats

The answer, it turns out, can be found in plate tectonics. Africa has been a hotbed of seismic activity for many millions of years. The Great Rift Valley, the Virunga Mountains chain of volcanoes and the Okavango Delta are all breathtaking evidence of a geological history of upheaval and turbulence. Biologists believe that the tigerfish were ultimately distributed so extensively by the movements of these massive continental tectonic plates, shifts that changed whole river courses, gradually transporting, fragmenting and isolating small populations of tigerfish into new areas and habitats. Over time, this isolation produced new species, now unable to mix with their ancestral populations and, even if they could, only able to successfully breed with their own kind.

At least one new tigerfish species evolved each time Africa suffered a massive geological event.

Using the latest genome-deciphering techniques, we can now fairly accurately work out when these evolutionary divisions occurred. It seems likely that at least one new tigerfish species evolved each time Africa suffered a massive geological event (bearing in mind that these happen gradually over many thousands of years). So, by ageing each species from their genetic differences we can tell approximately when these events happened and in what order.

It looks like tigerfish can help reveal Africa's geological past – quite an achievement for an obscure, scary-looking freshwater fish!

18

HOODWINKER SUNFISH

{Mola tecta}

A.K.A.

Schwimmender Kopf

SIZE

Up to 4.2 m (13 ft 9 in)

HABITAT

Southern Hemisphere

DISTINGUISHING FEATURES

Beak-like teeth

PERSONALITY

Predatory

LIKES

Sunbathing

SPECIAL SKILLS

Laying eggs

CONSERVATION STATUS

Not evaluated

N O SELF-RESPECTING BOOK on the amazing variety of fish forms would be complete if it neglected the marvellous, odd-shaped sunfish, which in many respects more resembles a futuristic diving bell or a spacecraft design than a fish. Weighing up to 1 tonne (2,205 lb), the ocean sunfish (*Mola mola*), related to the hoodwinker, is the heaviest bony fish on the planet. The biggest individuals can have a fin span of 4.2 m (13 ft 9 in), which is as tall as an elephant or wide as a London bus. Even so, sunfish look so comical and awkward, it's difficult to understand how they can survive at all. Once you've seen one, it will come as no surprise that sunfish have an exciting and unique lifestyle.

Along with the hoodwinker and the ocean sunfish (*M. mola*), which is the version most people recognize – not only because of it's unique looks but because it can be found throughout the temperate and tropical waters of every ocean on Earth – there is the southern hemisphere analogue known as the southern sunfish (*M. alexandrini*).

Lying in wait

The hoodwinker sunfish (which is the species I have illustrated here) is the most recently discovered member of the three-species family, having only been discovered very recently (though it's also hard to gauge how one might miss a surface-dwelling fish this big!). Most sunfish are only seen at sea unless one gets washed up a beach, as the type specimen of hoodwinker sunfish was in 2015 when it was stranded on a beach in Christchurch, New Zealand. Museum ichthyologists soon realized it was a new species, the first of its congeners to be discovered for 130 years. It was given the name of hoodwinker sunfish because it had remained cryptically hidden among populations of southern and ocean sunfish for so long (its scientific species name, *tecta*, translates as 'hidden' in Latin). It even occupies some of the same seas as its close relative, southern sunfish, being found off the coast of Australia, New Zealand, Chile and South Africa – so far!

Hoodwinker sunfish is the most dinner-plate-like of the three species, having a smoothly surfaced body with almost no bumps or

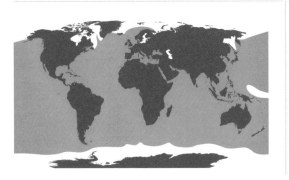

The biggest individuals can have a fin span as wide as a London bus.

depressions, unlike the other more well-known species. Still, sunfish are all rather strange looking due to their evolutionary pedigree. They are members of the same order as pufferfish and porcupinefish, both strange-looking creatures in their own right. The unusual flat, circular and plate-like body configuration of sunfish is generally thought of as being a fuel-efficient way of floating around using the ocean currents as transport. This free-floating lifestyle is all that is needed to find the jellyfish and salps (free-swimming translucent invertebrates, related to sea squirts and tunicates) they feed on. Salps are some of the simplest chordates in existence (the larger group that includes vertebrates such as sunfish and humans) and form what look like long strings of jelly floating aimlessly at the whims of the world's ocean currents – in many ways looking like giant oceanic frogspawn.

Sunfish lay the greatest number of eggs of any vertebrate.

Recently, more detailed studies have shown that the idea that sunfish are directionless, doing nothing but being dragged along by currents, is a fallacy. And, in fact, sunfish can be active predators, travelling vertically up and down the water column from the surface to hundreds of feet down, chasing squid, fish, crustaceans; they do take jellyfish and salps but that is by no means all of their diet.

Fast-growing leviathan

Probably the initial impression you will get from your first sighting of a sunfish is its size. To reach its bulk and length, you might think sunfish live for a long time and grow very slowly, as many other animals do to reach impressive sizes. However, a rescued living sunfish kept in Monterey Bay Aquarium in California grew from a 25-kg (55-lb) baby to a 400-kg (880-lb) monster in just over a year! That's an increase in size of sixteen times in the space of twelve months. Who would have guessed that jellyfish could be so filling? This was apparently not just a facet of it being fed frequently in captivity without oceanic space to move in; when the sunfish genome was studied, a gene sequence was identified that might be the key to the fish's highly rapid growth strategy. They have selected for genes closely involved with growth hormones and insulin production. It seems that there is an evolutionarily advantage for sunfish to grow rapidly, though we don't yet know why.

You may be wondering by now why fish of the genus *Mola* are called sunfish. They are neither yellow nor particularly hot, but what they do is float on the ocean's surface, basking in the sun; understandably, this is where most people randomly encounter them when sailing, and what has led to the idea that they just float around on the currents. This habit of sunbathing serves an essential purpose: sunfish need to warm up after a cold dive into the dark depths, and floating on their sides in the warm sunshine helps absorb the sun's heat rapidly while exposing the largest surface area to that radiation. Perhaps confusingly, some people call them moonfish, although up close they are often a ghostly white colour, so the name makes more immediate sense than sunfish. The German name for the fish is rather suggestive: *Schwimmender Kopf*; this translates as 'swimming head' and is a similar idea to the Polish name *samogłów* ('lonely head'); the Chinese take another tack and call them 'toppled wheel fish'.

Incredibly, sunfish also lay the greatest number of eggs of any vertebrate. It is estimated that they can produce as many as 300 million eggs at once. Not only that, they start life after hatching looking like a tiny cross between a pufferfish and a starfish while weighing no more than a grain of rice just a few millimetres long, despite ending up as one of the heaviest fish in the ocean: the increase in their body weight from fry to adult is more than 60 million times!

19

WOLF FISH

{Hoplias aimara}

A.K.A.

Anjumara

SIZE

Up to 1 m (3 ft 3 in)

HABITAT

South American rivers

DISTINGUISHING FEATURES

Shining eyes

PERSONALITY

Ambush hunter

LIKES

Darkness

SPECIAL SKILLS

Stealth attack

CONSERVATION STATUS

Not evaluated

HERE IS A giant that you might not have heard of: the wolf fish, also known as the anjumara. I had to include this species because it is just about one of my favourites of the lesser-known fish. When the wolf fish are out on the prowl at night, roaming the waterways of South America looking for food, it's a dangerous place to be. Even the piranhas take off and hide.

The first thing to note is that they are not really as fierce as wolves – they're perhaps a bit more like rottweilers or mastiffs – strong and powerful predators that are not afraid of almost anything. This fearlessness is perfectly demonstrated by the Trio Amerindians of Suriname in Central America, who catch wolf fish by making a splashing commotion at the edge of the water. The majority of fish tend to flee at the first sign of disturbance, but not wolf fish. In fact, the species often swims towards noise, believing it to be an animal

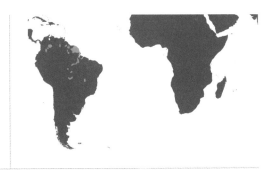

When the wolf fish are on the prowl, even the piranhas take off and hide.

in distress or another fish, opportunistically targeting the hapless animal for a meal. Of course, in this case, it usually ends with an arrow, but it does show just how pugnacious these fish can be.

A wolf out on its own

Wolf fish are voracious and, although predominantly fish hunters, they will attack almost anything from birds to snakes and lizards. I was told the story of a monkey that misjudged a jump and landed in the water right on the end of a branch; as it hit the water, a wolf fish took off its tail in one bite. The wolf fish has very sharp teeth (including some closely resembling canines on both top and bottom jaws) and extremely powerful bony jaws that operate almost like a bear trap. At first glance, their teeth don't look as frightening as piranhas' as they are hidden behind fleshy lips. Trust me, they are there.

The eeriest thing about wolf fish is the way that their eyes reflect light – somewhat similar to cats' eyes. When shining your torch along the river margins in a rainforest at evening, you will occasionally see two small red lights glowing back at you. Caiman (South America's answer to the crocodile, which is actually a crocodile) also have this feature, though the difference is that the reptile's eyes are usually above the water. While wolf fish are unlikely to kill you, their 3-cm- (1½-in-) long teeth can give you a nasty injury. Aquarists wear gloves when handling them, but they are prized as pets, though they understandably need a lot of space and care. Don't think that you will be safe keeping to the shallows. Wolf fish roam wherever they fancy, and if there were none in yesterday's paddling area, it doesn't mean there won't be some there today.

Lupine movements

The species makes annual migrations to breed when the rainy season hits their northern South American and Central American range from December to March when the rivers are at their most swollen (wolf fish are also found on the island of Trinidad). In Suriname, they head up creeks to breed, occasionally waiting at the mouths of these narrow waterways for enough water to build up. This freshwater migratory impulse is called being potamodromous (as opposed to anadromous, which describes fish that migrate downstream to saltwater, such as various species of salmon). Wolf fish can be quite territorial at this stage and are often found in very shallow water as the dry season takes hold and water levels in creeks drop. Water only ankle deep could be hiding a fish of some 23 kg (50 lb) or more; when one is disturbed, the sudden shock of the water erupting around you can be quite frightening.

Wolf fish vary in colour from slate black to a golden yellow tone, even between individuals in the same river. They sometimes

hide in underwater caves to rest and frequently startle people who are rooting around the riverbanks looking for other fish. Indigenous people often get a fright and can get bitten when attempting to get an easy meal of small catfish.

In Venezuela, wolf fish are reported to be found near waterfalls and rapids, but I have also found them in quite calm water, although that was during the day; so it's

Even fish that are caught in the same pool can vary massively in colour.

possible that the fish might rest up during the day, heading towards the rapids to hunt at night.

The hunter under threat

In some countries, such as French Guiana on the north Atlantic coast of South America, wolf fish can be the most common fish in a river system. Certainly, in parts of Suriname, it was possible to find them in huge schools but, as their meat is both delicious and not very bony, and they are not timid or much bothered by people splashing about making a noise, they are much sought after by fishermen. Huge numbers can be taken out with nets and traps in one go on the larger rivers, meaning that local populations can be decimated in a very short time.

Wolf fish are also facing another threat now: gold mining. This somewhat poorly regulated industry uses poisonous chemicals in the processes of extracting gold from rocks on site. These predominantly involve mercury – often the most polluting and damaging chemical that can be introduced into wild water systems. Mercury has a bad habit of remaining in the water table for a very long time, finding its way in minuscule amounts into the small invertebrates at the bottom of the food chain. When smaller fish eat these, they are in turn eaten by bigger fish, ultimately ending up in the apex predators such as wolf fish in huge, accumulated doses. A nasty twist is also that the many edible fish that mercury builds up in can also be eaten by humans, poisoning us in turn. Unfortunately, the staple diet of many rural indigenous people is fish. Mercury poisoning is horrific, having many physiological symptoms that can result in permanent neurological damage. The only real solution to this problem is the introduction of some kind of licencing and regulation – though often mining is done in some of the most remote and inaccessible places, poisoning rivers that run through several different countries, making it very hard to regulate.

Wolf fish are also facing another threat now: gold mining.

20

GIANT OCEANIC MANTA RAY

{Mobula birostris}

A.K.A.

Giant manta ray, oceanic manta ray, devilfish

SIZE

Up to 7 m (23 ft) across

HABITAT

Tropical and temperate waters worldwide

DISTINGUISHING FEATURES

Flying cape with horns

PERSONALITY

Intelligent, friendly

LIKES

Plankton

SPECIAL SKILLS

Spinning feeding manoeuvre

CONSERVATION STATUS

Endangered

THE GIANT OCEANIC manta ray is one of those fish most people can identify at first glance. It soars through the ocean's depths like a giant spacecraft. As we study its biology in order to understand it better, it also seems to be as full of secrets as Area 51.

Historically, manta rays were often called devilfish – although, so were gray whales, octopi and several other fish. This overused colloquial name derived from one of the ray's most distinctive physical attributes: two flaps or cephalic fins on the sides of their faces which resemble inwardly curved horns; these give them an 'evil' appearance. Manta rays are also black and resemble flying capes – *manta* means 'cloak' in Spanish and Portuguese.

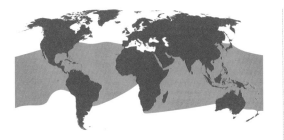

*It soars above the
ocean's depths in a
manner reminiscent
of a giant spacecraft.*

Underwater albatross

The three species of manta ray are the largest in the order Myliobatiformes and comprise their own family, the Mobulidae. Manta ray wingspans can grow to the very impressive size of 7 m (23 ft). By comparison, the wingspan of the largest bird, the royal albatross, reaches only a maximum of 3.7 m (12 ft).

Until 1987, one of their biggest secrets was that there were, in fact, two or three species of manta ray and not just one as previously believed. The largest is giant oceanic manta ray (as befits this section of the book) but the reef manta ray (*M. alfredi* – named after Prince Alfred, the Duke of Edinburgh) is a little smaller and more coastal in its habits. The reef manta ray was not finally confirmed as a separate species until 2009, despite being first described in 1848.

Trawling for plankton

Like many very large oceanic fish such as whale sharks (see pages 102–5) and basking sharks, manta rays feed on tons of some of the smallest life forms in the sea: plankton. The term 'plankton' is a catch-all for the complex mass of many tiny and often microscopic plants and animals, grouped under the terms 'phytoplankton' (comprised of photosynthetic algae) and 'zooplankton' (comprised of animals, particularly the larvae of starfish, crabs, fish and jellyfish). Plankton forms a dense and complex but highly nutritious living 'soup'

throughout the world's oceans, so populous that swathes of it can be seen from space. However, as a member of the planktonic community you are at the mercy of currents and upwellings. Due to this passivity, plankton swarms are often concentrated into vast,

Unlike many other species of ray, mantas have no spine in their tails.

extremely dense clouds with the consistency of a good broth. If a manta ray comes across such a bonanza, it performs a truly elegant feeding manoeuvre, throwing its mouth open and spinning around in circles to filter and scoop as much plankton as it can; it's the most effortless way of 'stuffing your face' I can think of! Once full, the ray glides imperiously away to digest its meal.

The dangers of diving

Despite their awesome bulk, manta rays are often kept in aquaria and even seem comfortable in the presence of humans. This is perhaps an indication of a creature with a level of intelligence beyond most other fish, and biologists have indeed discovered that manta rays have the largest brains of their kind. This tolerance of people is sometimes a boon for underwater tourism. Properly managed and planned, such tourism can be a big incentive for conservation and deliver advantages for both us and the manta rays.

The greatest danger of this kind of 'exploitation' is its very popularity. In the South Pacific French Polynesian island of Bora Bora, a well-known group of manta rays had been habituated and were a 'sure thing' for a popular night dive, replete with the thrill of these giant fish swooshing over your head mere feet away. However, as more and more people wanted to experience this spectacle and were prepared to pay large amounts of money for it, the mantas couldn't cope and many of the fish have now deserted the area due to excessive disturbance.

The manta rays are still there, but the industry is not what it was.

Even so, manta ray tourism is a lot better than some of the other interactions with humans. These huge and wonderful creatures have recently become a target of the Chinese medicine plague (though, despite having 2,000-year-old roots, there is nothing very 'traditional' about much of it). The gill rakers are alleged to have healing properties and fisheries in Madagascar, Philippines, Indonesia and Pakistan, and anywhere else where the fish remain unprotected, are being overexploited to feed the market.

Saving the giants

The good news is that many governments are trying to inhibit the killing. The Maldives led the way in 1995, with Mexico following in 2007, and the Philippines and Hawaii falling into line in 2009, but the legislation is still difficult to enforce in such a lucrative and underground industry. The creation of large marine sanctuaries is perhaps the best news: manta rays thrive in such areas and many people are prepared to travel and enjoy them.

The damage done every year to manta ray populations is exacerbated by the fact that manta rays are very slow breeders. They tend to only have one or two pups at a time – and one is standard. Pregnancy lasts for a whole year – a period as long as some of the longest gestating mammals like Grant's zebra. This begins with the eggs being fertilized internally in her womb by a swarm of ardent admirers. Interestingly, these suitors form a single-file queue as they chase the female through the mid-ocean waters, while she releases sex pheromones into the water to drive them wild. A nutritious oxygenated secretion similar to milk is produced by the female's womb to feed the youngster until it is born a year later. The pup emerges into the world swaddled in its own wings and, once in the water, it spreads them for the first time before immediately soaring off into the blue yonder as a perfect replica of its parents.

Manta rays are very amenable to being kept in aquaria.

21

GIANT OARFISH

{Regalecus glesne}

A.K.A.

Pacific oarfish, king
of herrings, ribbonfish,
streamer fish

SIZE

Up to 8 m (26 ft)

HABITAT

Open ocean

**DISTINGUISHING
FEATURES**

Red dorsal fin

PERSONALITY

Unknown

LIKES

Krill

SPECIAL SKILLS

Vertical movement

**CONSERVATION
STATUS**

Least Concern

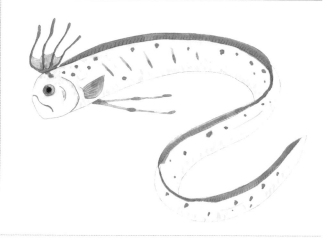

THE ASTONISHINGLY WEIRD, wonderful and enormous giant oarfish is the perfect candidate for this chapter. It is certainly a giant among fish, but just big they are is difficult to assess. Human encounters with the bizarre giant oarfish are almost invariably with dead or dying individuals that have either washed ashore or have been found at sea, floating on the surface; so it is a rare and lucky event to see one in its prime. It also holds a key place in human culture: there is little doubt that its long, bulky but tapering form is the source of our mythological legends of sea serpents. Its lengthy, sinuous body is enough to inspire those tales, while its eye-catching rooster-like crown of red fins on the top of its head only adds to its unique appearance. It is reported to reach up to 11 m (36 ft) in length, though official records state no more than 8 m (26 ft). A giant oarfish's body is very thin and tapering and it has a wavy dorsal fin along its entire length, a long, red filamentous headdress and two similar long pelvic fins that almost hide two adjacent stubby pectoral fins – these almost certainly gave the fish its name, as they could be taken to resemble oars.

In Japanese folklore, its close relative the Russell's oarfish (*R. russellii*), a deep water species, is believed to be a messenger from the sea god Ryūjin's palace. In Japanese mythology, if seen, it is a warning of an approaching cataclysmic event such as a tsunami or an earthquake. When several were encountered washed ashore or caught in nets a few years before the dreadful events at Fukushima, when a serious accident occurred at the Daiichi Nuclear Power Plant after an earthquake created a massive tsunami in 2011, a few superstitious people connected the two events. As yet, there is no real scientific evidence to prove that oarfish respond to seismic activity, but we do know that many species of fish are very sensitive to such occurrences – so there may be a little truth behind the legends.

Rowing upwards not forwards

A lot of speculation surrounds the purpose of the oarfish's bizarre pelvic fins, which can be seen as two long filaments on the underside at the front end of the body. In earlier times, sailors believed that the fish swam using these paired fins like oars to propel themselves

It is a vanishingly rare opportunity to see a giant oarfish in its prime.

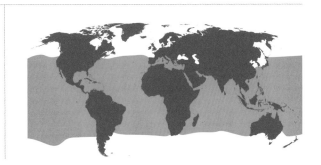

through the water; no matter how unlikely that sounds, this theory is what gave the oarfish its name. But all guesswork about how they swim was put to one side in 2010, when an oarfish was seen alive and well and in motion for the first time in history.

The SERPENT project (an acronym for 'Scientific and Environmental ROV – Remote Operated Vehicle – Partnership Using Existing Industrial Technology'), which operates in the Gulf of Mexico, set out to utilize underwater technology from several different disciplines (though mainly from the oil and mining industries, which invest in lots of this kind of kit) to observe underwater life and make new discoveries, if possible. One of the mysteries they solved has been the secret of how oarfish move. They captured what was then unique footage of a healthy giant oarfish in its natural surroundings in the Gulf of Mexico, swimming in the mesopelagic layer of the open sea – the twilight zone between the dark ocean depths and the sunlit upper water column. It was first noted at a depth of 460 m (about 1,500 ft), not swimming horizontally using its sinuous body like an eel, but rather moving vertically; that is, with its head pointing to the surface and its tail pointing down into the depths.

Most land-based creatures exist in one plane with our feet on the ground, enabling us to move forwards, backwards or sideways, left and right. Almost all fish, however, live in a more three-dimensional world where they can move in all of the ways we can but also have to

The oarfish looks like it was designed by a four-year-old, but it is very real.

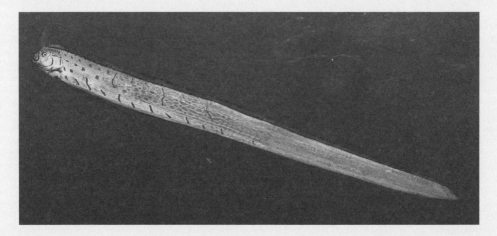

deal with up and down as well – much as birds can in the air. Oarfish exploit this ability fully by having evolved to largely move up and down. In a way, oarfish claimed a niche all of their own, moving like elevators in the deep ocean, ingesting all the small fish, krill and other pelagic crustaceans they can along the way – a very economical and energy-conserving way of moving and eating.

Sinuous motion

The SERPENT footage also revealed in some detail how oarfish swim – and it's not with their small, oar-like pelvic fins, which were not seen to be involved in locomotion at all. All along an oarfish's back is the most delicate and pronounced dorsal fin, starting just behind the eye and running unbroken right down to the tail. This is helpfully highlighted in bright red and easy to observe and film. The dorsal fin allows an oarfish to swim almost without moving, as it undulates in a perfect wave that can be directed forwards and backwards to allow the fish to manoeuvre up and down. The other fins are held out like the pole of a tightrope walker, though whether they are used for balance or directionally, or even just being held out of the way, is a mystery, like so much of the oarfish's life.

The dorsal fin allows an oarfish to swim almost without moving.

Giant oarfish hold the record for the longest bony fish on the planet (whale sharks being cartilaginous). Photographs of US Navy SEALs holding up stranded individuals will give you a real sense of their true size (a search on the internet should produce some of these). The giant oarfish is believed to be oceanodromous – that is, it follows its food sources around the ocean and is mainly found in tropical and mid-latitude waters across the whole globe. It ranges through the mesopelagic zone down to about 1,000 m (about 3,300 ft).

Despite the fish's legendary reputation and size, you are only ever likely to see one after it has washed up on the shore, unless of course you are a submarine captain.

22

ARAPAIMA

{Arapaima gigas}

A.K.A.

Pirarucu

SIZE

Often over 2 m (7 ft)

HABITAT

South American rivers

DISTINGUISHING FEATURES

Large scaled armour

PERSONALITY

Immovable

LIKES

Will eat leftovers on the water surface

SPECIAL SKILLS

Breathing surface air

CONSERVATION STATUS

Insufficient data

As its huge back rises out of the water the first time you spot it, this appears to be not so much a fish as an island. As can often happen in the small, muddy oxbow lakes or shallow river sections of the Amazon Basin, you might think to yourself that you have just seen a monster – but in reality, you will have seen what may arguably be the largest freshwater fish on the planet. There are some very big Russian sturgeon (*Acipenser gueldenstaedtii*) in Central Asia and catfish – for example, the lau lau or piraíba (*Brachyplatystoma filamentosum*), found in the same rivers, which can grow as large as a small great white shark. Even the occasional big bull shark will cruise a river, so let us justify that claim by stating that arapaima averages the largest freshwater species on Earth: whereas one or two outlying individuals from other species might top the scales as larger, most adult arapaima will be bigger.

The genus *Arapaima* has been around for hundreds of thousands of years. They look like ancient life forms,

too, resembling fishy dinosaurs up close with their large, bony-plated heads, tiny eyes and nostrils, and vast bony full-body scales that appear as if they have been individually crafted by an expert carver. They are surprisingly easy to find because they frequently come up to breathe air. Every few minutes, up to half an hour, they break the surface and take a massive gulp of oxygen. They aren't holding their breath like you and me, as they can still derive adequate oxygen from the water around them, but the arapaima tops up its air with a simple 'lung' enabling it to sustain its breathing in water low in oxygen. It's quite the sight to see.

Ancient appeal

Arapaima are deep-bodied, with wide, thick scales, the colours of which can vary from river to river, territory to territory, from shiny greenish blue to dark chocolate with crimson edges. Historically, all arapaima from Guyana to Brazil to Ecuador were understood to be the same species, but this extreme colour variation finally inspired ichthyologists to look a little closer. Analysis of hundreds of DNA samples from museum specimens soon revealed that there were up to five species in the genus *Arapaima*. Each was easily as distinctive as the different species of elephant found in the Old World.

What they all have in common is the knack of living in oxygen-poor water – very useful in the Amazon with its cycles of boom and bust during the rainy and dry seasons every year. By their habitual gulping of air, the fish can get oxygen into their systems even in cloying, oxygen-poor water with near-zero visibility. As the pools dry, though, the fish can become quite vulnerable to being stranded, and there are stories of massive arapaima trapped in rapidly receding jungle pools being snatched and wrestled to the banks above by aggressive, hungry jaguars. This is just about the only animal capable of getting through the thick armoured scales of arapaima with its teeth, which can also bite through a turtle shell with little effort.

Crushing and voracious

Though largely carnivorous, feeding on other fish, insects, crustaceans and small land mammals straying into the water, arapaima also eat seeds and fruit. Even so, unlike some of the big-toothed fish that they live among, they actually have rather unimpressive teeth. However, what they lack in dentistry they make up for with power. Arapaima crush their prey with their hard bony mouths and also are reputed to hunt in an unusual and somewhat bizarre way.

Occasionally on a remote oxbow lake, you might hear what sounds like a gunshot echo out.

I have personally observed what might be the arapaima's hunting technique in the wild. Occasionally on a remote oxbow lake (these can be miles in length in the Amazon), you might hear what sounds like a gunshot echo out. This cracking sound, which could easily be mistaken for lightning or a high-velocity rifle, is an arapaima slapping the surface of the water so powerfully that it creates a loud smack or shot-like sound. It's almost like the sound killer whales make with their tails at sea. Arapaima are believed to sometimes use this technique to corral local fish into huge shoals and then stun them en masse by whipping their tails into the groups of fish – this tail slapping has been filmed causing a huge splash of water on the surface. It is probable that they then hoover up their stunned and floating victims before they come round again. It is also possible that the arapaima are communicating with one another with this extraordinary sound to solve territorial disputes, somewhat in the way that humpback whales do at sea. Either explanation for this behaviour is possible, but the jury is out, waiting for scientists or filed observers to solve the mystery.

Rocket launcher

The real tragedy of arapaima is that they taste delicious and are so huge that they can feed an entire village once caught. In Brazil, arapaima have unfortunately been hunted out of many of the rivers they once inhabited. Despite their popularity as food, hunting for arapaima is not for the faint-hearted. If they feel disturbed, the fish launch themselves out of the water like Exocet missiles. If you consider that their heads are thicker than most sledgehammers, and almost as hard and weighty, you can grasp how easily they can split wooden boats in half, as well as regularly breaking bones and destroying camera equipment.

Arapaima are most active at night, moving out of their muddy territories under trees in lakes or lagoons or on the edge of the rivers and cruising purposefully into the main channel of a river, patrolling it, looking for shoals of sleeping or resting fish.

Arapaima's scales can vary in colour from river to river.

They are now endangered and only a few places on Earth can declare themselves sanctuaries to these incredible fish, which probably once spooked the odd dinosaur in the shallows. There is something inevitable and substantial about them that is hard to grasp. They are solid and dynamic like time or sand and – like all of the fish in this book – the world is a better place with them in it.

23

WHALE SHARK

{Rhincodon typus}

A.K.A.

Vaame (Swahili), *pez dama* (Spanish) – which translates as 'the lady fish'

SIZE

Around 13 m (42 ft)

HABITAT

Open ocean

DISTINGUISHING FEATURES

300 rows of tiny teeth

PERSONALITY

Gentle giant

LIKES

Plankton and krill

SPECIAL SKILLS

Disappearing

CONSERVATION STATUS

Endangered

It's hard to comprehend the immense size of this species, by far the biggest fish in the world – perhaps the only way to grasp their enormity is to get in the water with one and see for yourself. However, this should not be encouraged in anything but the right circumstances; these gentle, filter-feeding giants are endangered species and largely protected from intentional human disturbance.

The average size of a fully grown whale shark is approximately 13 m (42 ft) in length, weighing in at around 9 tonnes (20,000 lb). Such a huge animal is not hard to spot, but despite this, we know surprisingly little about them. Almost all our information is from random field observations and anecdotal recollections.

Even their size is generally only estimated; stranded individuals are unsupported by the water and tend to sag, giving a false idea of their living bulk, while whale sharks in the ocean are moving and therefore make it very difficult to get a precise reading or measurement of their size. In recent years, there has been some progress in employing laser photogrammetry for more accurate readings.

With big things, people love to exaggerate. Certainly, some sizeable whale sharks have been reported over the years but the anecdotal sighting I feel most comfortable reporting is a true monster that tragically washed ashore in Ratnagiri, off the south-west Indian coast on 30 September 1995, that allegedly measured 20.78 m (68 ft 1 in). This fish would have blocked an entire Olympic running track and was twice the length of a London red bus. In fact, a Learjet 35 is shorter at 17.7 m (58 ft) and can seat fifteen people comfortably.

Wandering giants

Another reason the species is so difficult to study is its penchant for nomadism. It rarely stays in the same place for very long and a whale shark off the coast of Mexico can be in Tonga, Polynesia, a couple of months later, while one off the coast of East Africa could eventually be cruising around Thailand over the same period of time. These are not random statements; both situations happened when scientists radio-tagged whale sharks and both involved round trips of about 13,000 km (8,078 miles).

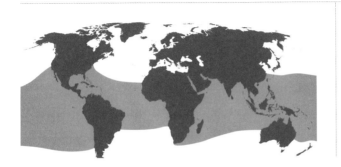

It's hard to comprehend the immense size of this species.

Plumbing the depths

The species is not only a long-distance traveller but can also dive to great depths: dives of up to 1,928 m (6,325 ft or 1.2 miles) have been recorded (with the deepest diver being a juvenile), enabling individuals to disappear entirely from sight and making this giant even harder to find at times. They are far from predictable and incredibly hard to pin down. In 2011, a huge gathering of 400 whale sharks amassed off the Yucatán coast of Mexico in what was described as the greatest assembly of the species ever. It has never been repeated as far as we know – although that might have had something to do with the large numbers of tourists that invaded the area to 'free dive' with them. Whale sharks are a lot more sensitive to their surroundings than one might realize and human disturbance can soon see the sharks disappear – or even not show up if they detect human presence.

Whale shark longevity is also only estimated at present, though it is believed these fish could live as long as 130 years. Unlike sunfish (see pages 82–5) which grow extremely quickly for a fish their size, little is known of the time it takes a whale shark to mature – mainly because the fry are rarely seen and consequently difficult to monitor. In 2020, an attempt was made to calculate the ages of whale sharks using carbon-dating techniques. It was determined with some confidence that a 10-m (33-ft) female could

A single Chinese factory processed 600 whale and basking sharks for their meat and fins.

potentially be around fifty years old. This suggests that whale sharks take an exceedingly long time to reach sexual maturity – perhaps thirty years or more. There is not much current information about the gestation period of a whale shark, either, or how long or where they mate. In fact, one of the natural history holy grails is to find the breeding grounds of whale sharks to film a birth. A recent report from the World Wide Fund for Nature in the Philippines logged 168 sightings in 2019, with many claiming to be 'juveniles, indicating that this region could be a focus of future exploration and research. Stay tuned.

The mysteries of birth

In terms of breeding, the only verified report we have is of a big pregnant female that was accidentally caught in a fishery in Taiwan and then died. A post-mortem revealed she had 304 young whale sharks inside her. Whether they are all born at the same time, and when and where they give birth, are still mysteries for the most part.

You'd think that being so big would preclude most whale sharks from the attentions of predators, but there is one to which they are certainly not immune: that of humans. An undercover report from Australia in 2016 revealed that a single Chinese factory processed 600 whale and basking sharks for their meat and fins to be sold for food (with the latter mostly for shark's fin soup); it doesn't stop there – the skin and oil are sent to North America and Europe (the former to be tanned for bags and shoes, the latter to be included in vitamin and health supplements). Without knowing much of the fundamentals of the whale shark life cycle, it's very hard to know if any part of that industry and trade is sustainable. The whale shark is officially listed as endangered by the International Union for Conservation of Nature (IUCN, 'the global authority on the status of the natural world and the measures needed to safeguard it'), but the species has the misfortune of spending much of its life in waters where there is little observation or policing. Whale sharks are monitored by the Conservation of Migratory Sharks (CMS), along with manta rays and great white sharks.

Whale sharks can be so large that a whole village of remoras can ride along without them noticing.

With such a slow growth rate, late sexual maturity and hard-to-establish breeding habits and distribution, it remains difficult to understand how to best preserve this planet's whale shark population. Hopefully, there is enough ongoing research to answer such questions and keep these benevolent giants around for generations to come.

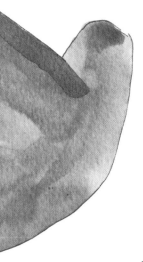

— Chapter 4 —

STRANGER THINGS

I've reserved this category of fish for the strangest denizens of the deep. To be honest, nature doesn't fundamentally consider anything strange; most evolution has a purpose and that elephant-like nose or hammer-like head is often the key to a species' survival, making it impossible to live without. Come with me, now, into the weirdest waters and sample the extremes of fish form and function. Though, on consideration, many of the other fish in this book could be included among the strangest, too!

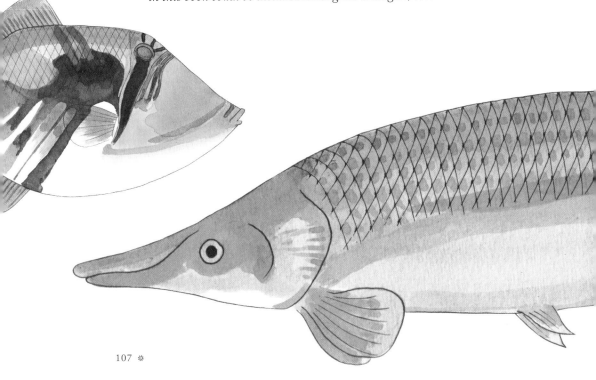

24

PETER'S ELEPHANTNOSE FISH

{Gnathonemus petersii}

AFTER THE STICKLEBACK, this is the best-named fish on Earth. This bizarre African creature is named after German naturalist Wilhelm Peters, who spent much of his career exploring, describing and documenting the wildlife of Mozambique, Angola and West Africa in the early to mid nineteenth century for the Berlin Museum. This fish with its striking proboscis is not the only thing named in his honour; he also has a large bay in Greenland named after him.

Despite its odd sound, it didn't take much imagination to come up with the name for this fish: it does have a nose like an elephant. This is probably one of the most unusual-looking fish species on the planet. However, its nominal 'nose' isn't really for breathing and manipulating objects like an elephant's trunk, but is actually a handily adapted bottom lip – though, if anything, it is more tactile than an elephant's trunk, as we will see.

Electric elephant

Elephantnoses are one of the few animals that can generate electrical currents. They use the electricity they generate to navigate around the more dark and secretive underwater zones of West African rivers, particularly the Congo Basin and its right-bank tributary, the Ubangi River. These waters are often snarled up with debris and mud, making it very hard for a standard fish to find its way around – but elephantnoses (family Mormyridae) have evolved one of the more extreme adaptations to ensure their survival in such clouded waters. The Ubangi mormyrid or long-nosed elephantfish, as it is otherwise called, possesses what is known as a *Schnauzeorgan* (which means 'nose organ' in German, of course) – an appendage that is covered in electroreceptors that allow the fish to detect the weak electrical fields that are produced by other animals; the rest of its body also has a healthy complement of these sensitive electrolocators. Electroreceptors are also present in other aquatic animals, such as the lemon shark, the electric eel (see pages 34–7) and the Guiana dolphin, as well as mammals such as the platypus and echidnas and even some airborne insects such as honey bees.

Radar eyes

With this radar-like technology to help find its way around its mud-clouded native rivers and its nocturnal habits, Peter's elephantnose fish effectively spends most of its time in the dark; because of this,

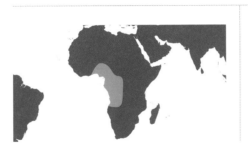

Its nominal 'nose' is actually a handily adapted top lip.

you might think it had forsaken its other senses. If you have parking sensors on your car, why bother looking where you are going? It also has a sclerotic-looking layer over its eyes, and for many years scientists had considered the fish to be almost blind. However, it was recently discovered that it is 'differently visioned' rather than blind and, in fact, at certain light bandwidths, the species can see better than almost any other living thing on Earth.

That might seem to be a bold claim. Human eyesight is relatively good, and our eyes have rods and cones – the former for using low light and the latter for brightness, working together so that we can see well in a variety of natural conditions. Many animals see better in near-pitch darkness than us, but overall human eyesight is a pretty useful system. Peter's elephantnose fish also has a similar arrangement of rods and cones, but they also have something else. That weird, apparently atrophied, layer over their eyes

The species has evolved the largest brain-to-weight ratio of any animal in the world.

turns out to be composed of hundreds of small, cup-like depressions, formed of crystals growing on their retinas. These crystals are made of guanine – also found in the scales of the alligator gar (see pages 116–19) – which amplifies the available light, sending it into their eyes to the incredible number of rods and cones in the retina.

Big bold brains

Not only this, but the species has also evolved the largest brain-to-weight ratio of any animal in the world. Biologists measuring the amount of oxygen our brains and bodies use have found that the brain-to-body oxygen consumption of most animals is in the region of about 2–8 per cent. Concurrently, the brain uses around 2–8 per cent of the entire body's oxygen intake for its major functions (which include thoughts, movement, eating and digesting, as examples). In humans, however the brain consumes about 20 per cent of the oxygen

They are one of the few fish that can swim backwards.

that our body uses – that probably makes sense owing to our self-awareness and unique ability to involve the brain in problem-solving and creativity, meaning that our brains need extra energy to process all the complex information involved. As I write, my brain is working overtime coping with the dexterity of my fingers, accessing the information I'm writing about and enabling me to think about what I write next, not to mention considering whether what I'm writing makes sense and the background hum of emotions and feelings. Unsurprisingly, we use a lot of oxygen for our brains when juggling all these tasks. However, one species uses more: Peter's elephantnose fish uses three times as much oxygen as the human brain. Despite being no bigger than a banana, this freshwater fish species dedicates 60 per cent of its oxygen intake to feed brain function.

This fish can see in blinding sunlight and abysmal darkness equally, as well as being able to accurately judge distances, distinguish different shapes and materials in extreme conditions, and determine whether objects are alive or dead just by looking at them. One recent study discovered that they might also be able to see in colour where there is none. Different types of food generate different colours to which the fish respond – and you can trick them into trying to eat something that isn't food if you make it the appropriate colour. Peter's elephantnose fish is, in fact, the opposite of blind, and has the unique ability to keep processing much more information than even our huge brains.

25

PICASSO
TRIGGERFISH

{Rhinecanthus aculeatus}

A.K.A.

Lagoon triggerfish, *humuhumunuku-nukuāpu'a*

SIZE

Around 15 cm (6 in)

HABITAT

Shallow reefs

DISTINGUISHING FEATURES

Beak-like mouth

PERSONALITY

Aggressive

LIKES

Crabs, shrimps, lobsters and sea urchins

SPECIAL SKILLS

Wedging itself in crevices

CONSERVATION STATUS

Not evaluated

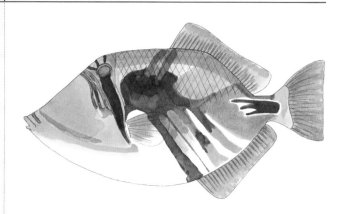

THE PICASSO TRIGGERFISH is also known as the lagoon triggerfish, but it's hard to imagine that even that great artist himself could have designed such extraordinary colours and patterns. In fact, the species was the inspiration for this entire book. At the start, I wanted to show people that something so outlandish and seemingly over the top could exist on this planet naturally. Although the strange birds, amphibians, reptiles and mammals of the Earth are perhaps more well-known, nothing in nature beats the remarkable variety and diversity of fish, typified by this ocean species.

Diamond in the rough

Firstly, I should point out what a bizarre shape the triggerfish has: diamond-shaped in profile, with a small beak-like mouth and tiny eye – but with a whole-body pattern that pleasingly enables me to use every colour on my palette and run wild with it. It is known as the blackbar triggerfish in South Africa and – as colourfully as its pattern – *humuhumunukunukuāpu'a* (which translates as 'the fish with a nose like a pig' or humu humu for short) in Hawaii, where the lagoon triggerfish's close relative, the reef trigger (*R. rectangulus*), is the state fish. Picasso is still my favourite. Either way, It's not possible to ignore a fish like this – it demands attention.

Triggerfish are quite well known for their aggression. They're the piscean equivalent of terriers, as they are no more than 30 cm (12 in) in length but behave as if they have much more power and sway than they appear to have. Especially when they are breeding. The females will chase and bite almost any other creature that gets too close – and that includes divers and snorkellers. According to one source, a lagoon triggerfish will defend its breeding territory by swimming upwards in a cone-shaped direction emanating from its nest – this means that, if you swim up to get away, then you are just staying in the danger zone, so it is more advisable to swim away rather than up to avoid painful harassment. Respect its wishes and retreat to a safer distance. If it's a titan triggerfish (*Balistoides viridescens*) you will have 75 cm (30 in) of parrot-beaked attack heading in your direction, so use this information to avoid all triggerfish, if you're on a dive.

The females will chase and bite almost any other creature that gets too close.

Crab shell-crackers

Even a small lagoon triggerfish can administer a nasty bite. This is because they dine out on some of the toughest-shelled animals on the reef (which also accounts for the unusual shape). Triggerfish love crabs, shrimps, lobsters and sea urchins – all creatures that have more body armour than a medieval knight. Those small but powerful jaws are refined to crack shells and break up those hard-earned defences while keeping the rest of the fish's face out of harm's way.

Triggerfish are extremely territorial, and once they have established themselves, they can usually be found swimming around these territories for several years afterwards – which makes them popular dive spots. Being bigger, male triggerfish defend a much larger territorial area than females and often keep several females (each with a territory) within his own, in a manner suggestive of a complex Venn diagram; the female territories don't quite overlap but sometimes almost touch each other while the males cover all of them. When it's time to breed, the male will mate with each female inside his range, after which she will lay the eggs and guard them as they develop. This is when the species becomes most aggressive.

Their unusual double cone seems to work in a very similar way to human eyesight.

Triggers in their fins

The name 'triggerfish' does not come from their tendency to leap to 'attack mode', but from an even more dangerous anatomical feature. Triggerfish have a long, vicious and sharp spine at the front of their dorsal fins which they use in defence. Their strategy is to swim into a coral crevice or gap in the reef and, once safely wedged inside, deploy its spine to lock itself in place, making it virtually impossible for a predator to remove. Most predators (reef sharks and groupers) will be immediately put off or will, at least, give up rather quickly. The weird thing is that there are two dorsal spines; the larger one cannot be 'put away' until the second, smaller spine has been sheathed. This is why they are called 'triggerfish': the fish has to have its 'trigger' set before becoming dangerous.

New ways of seeing

Bright colours can be seen everywhere on a coral reef; logically, you'd think being able to see most of them would be important. However, recent studies of the lagoon triggerfish have shown that they have a rather unusual collection of cones in their eyes (cones being the photoreceptor cells in the retinas of animal and our eyes that determine colour). Humans have three types of cone that each work on a major part of the colour spectrum: blue, green and red. Triggerfish have just two kinds of cone (a single cone and a joined-up double cone), which made many scientists believe that colour vision was not possible. However, this idea was destroyed by a recent laboratory experiment in which some triggerfish were trained to recognize colours by rewarding them with food when they picked the right colour. It showed that the unusual double cone seems to work in a very similar way to human eyesight. Put simply, triggerfish can see trichromatically. This is a remarkable discovery where supposedly 'primitive' fish are concerned.

The forty species of triggerfish are found right across the oceans of the tropics, from the eastern Atlantic to South Africa, and from the Indo-Pacific to the southern coast of Japan, and even as far south as New Caledonia. Where there is warmth and a reef you will be likely to find a triggerfish's cone-shaped territory. The Picasso triggerfish is one of the most common and widespread and well worth seeing – just don't get too close!

Even head-on, they are one of the most striking fish on our planet.

26 ALLIGATOR GAR

{Atractosteus spatula}

A.K.A.

Garpike, garfish

SIZE

Around 1.8 m (6 ft)

HABITAT

Lakes and reservoirs

DISTINGUISHING FEATURES

Extra-tough scales

PERSONALITY

Ambush predator

LIKES

Fish, birds or crabs

SPECIAL SKILLS

Breathing with a lung-like bladder

CONSERVATION STATUS

Least Concern

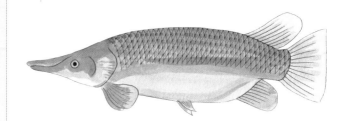

'PREHISTORIC' IS AN adjective often bandied around to describe the more antediluvian-looking animals of the world; when used in the case of this striking fish species, it's much more appropriate than most. Alligator gar are huge freshwater fish, though they do occasionally stray into brackish water near the coast. Once distributed throughout the USA, it is now limited to the southern states and ubiquitous in the Mississippi River, along with bayous, bays, lakes and rivers from Texas to Alabama.

Alligator gar was once fairly common, but in the days before we more fully understood the fragility of ecosystems, these primeval-looking monsters were labelled 'trash fish' and fishermen and waterways management were essentially given an open licence for their destruction. What wasn't appreciated was that can't remove a large apex predator from a wetland or river system without it having a massive knock-on impact on all of the animals and plants that live in the same

These primeval-looking monsters were once labelled 'trash fish'.

rivers and lakes. Ironically, the species is currently being reintroduced into areas that are now overrun by invasive introduced species, such as the east Siberian and Chinese silver carp (*Hypophthalmichthys molitrix*). You might have seen videos of people on speedboats being attacked by leaping fish whose defensive response to noise is to power out of the water; these are silver carp. If the gar had been left alone in these lakes and rivers, then these acrobatic torpedos might not have got such a stronghold – however, humans do tend to learn such ecological lessons after the horses have not only bolted, but been gone for so long that we almost forgot we had horses.

Alligator ambush

Alligator gar are ambush predators, hanging effortlessly just below the surface of the water like a half-submerged log, then striking suddenly, as soon as a fish, crawdad or water bird edges into range. They are equipped with a mouthful of crocodile-sharp teeth – so once they have got a grip on their prey, death is usually a 'done deal'.

It certainly is shaped like a predator: with torpedo-like proportions and a broad, sweeping tail able to generate a sprinter's start. Alligator gar fins are 'heterocercal', which means that their tail fins are not symmetrical, and the spine grows up inside the top lobe, lengthening the tail and enabling its use as an underwater sail. This is not unique to gars – however, two traits, in particular, do stand out: it has the most extraordinary scales and is also able to breathe air, in a manner like no other fish.

That osprey is lucky to have got out of the way of a flying gar. I am not sure who would have got the bigger surprise.

Alligator gar scales are made from one of the toughest natural materials on Earth; scientists have to use drills to be able to penetrate them when tagging these creatures. The scales are rhomboid in shape and composed of a material called ganoid, which has an external layer similar to the enamel on your teeth. So remarkable are these scales that Native Americans used them for arrowheads, as well as employing alligator gar skins to make leather and protect their plows. This incredible evolutionary quirk – only shared by four other piscean oddities: sturgeons, paddlefishes, bowfins and bichirs – is being thoroughly researched by biologists and engineers alike. Could the scales of this seemingly prehistoric fish with a face like an alligator hold the secret to the evolution of our teeth? And could this durable material be adapted to more human needs than arrowheads?

Breathing with a bladder

Alligator gar also breathe air. This in itself is not unique among fish as, like all other fish, gars have gills – but they also have an air bladder replete with innumerate tiny blood vessels that enables the gar to take in air, almost like a lung. Not only does this function aid buoyancy – that is, after all, the purpose of the swim bladder in every fish – but it is also used to oxygenate the blood. This adaptation means that the fish can live in the almost anaerobic water conditions in which most other fish would suffocate in minutes. The gar's physiology has evolved to cope with a fluctuating world of floods and droughts – so much so, that even the largest gar can survive in a muddy puddle. A very atmospheric way of seeing this species in action is to visit Louisiana and wait for a perfect, still summer evening to take a small boat out on a lake. With the slight breeze tickling your hair, all around you will hear the explosive gulps and splashes of alligator gars – some that could weigh 45 kg (100 lb) or be 3 m (10 ft) long, as they take in noisy and copious gulps of air. It's certainly some sight to see!

The gar's ability to cope with ever-changing environmental conditions does not much affect their breeding cycle, which is closely tied to the seasons. It waits until all the conditions are just right: sunlight, day length, temperature and water levels and depth must combine in the perfect trigger of mating behaviour. The spring floods that break the rivers from their usual constraints and overflow into neighbouring meadows and grasslands are exactly what the fish are waiting for. Only then, like a swarm of prehistoric water beasts, do they pour into these water meadows en masse. Jostling and shoving against each other with a rattling and scraping of scaly armour, the gars stick multitudes of red eggs to the stems of the grass and other plants, for eggs to grow safely and hatch away from the predators that remain trapped in main rivers. However, unlike the eggs of other ganoid-scaled fish species such as sturgeons, the alligator gar's eggs are no delicacy: they are, in fact, poisonous to humans.

> *Even the largest gar can survive in a muddy puddle.*

How large a gar can grow is an ongoing debate, although I suspect that there are as-yet undiscovered monsters still out there. The largest recorded so far got tangled up in a commercial fishing net in Lake Chotard, a water body that straddles the state lines of Louisiana and Mississippi. This mega-fish measured 2.6 m (8 ft 5 in), had a girth of 119 cm (47 in) and weighed 148.3 kg (327 lb) – this thoroughly dwarfed the previous rod-caught record – recorded in 1958 in Texas – of 125.6 kg (279 lb). There may well be more careful giants still out there, avoiding the nets, traps and hooks.

27

FANFIN ANGLER

{Caulophryne jordani}

A.K.A.

Hairy anglerfish

SIZE

Females: up to 20 cm
(8 in)

HABITAT

Deep ocean

**DISTINGUISHING
FEATURES**

A mass of fins and
tentacles

PERSONALITY

Loner

LIKES

Fishing

SPECIAL SKILLS

Bioluminscence

**CONSERVATION
STATUS**

Least Concern

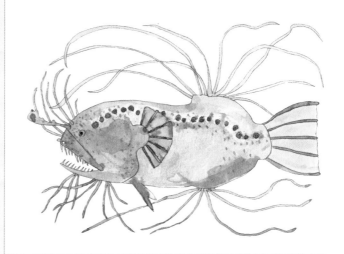

A LIVING NIGHTMARE – not just to look at but to try to paint as well – this grotesque species is almost ludicrously ugly enough to make William Blake and Hieronymous Bosch look like they weren't even trying. However, what it lacks in aesthetics, the anglerfish gains in purpose. When you dwell in the deepest darkness of the ocean, looks are irrelevant – to survive down there takes a certain kind of fish.

Anglerfish are famous, mostly because of their fishing techniques, as the name suggests. They are fish that fish for fish and go about their business with equipment that would befit any human angler in similar circumstances. Fanfin anglers have a fishing

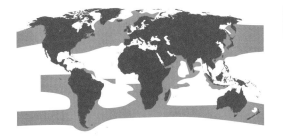

Only deep-sea anglerfish have the famous 'light-up' or bioluminescent lures.

lure balanced on the top of their heads – actually a part of the dorsal (or top) fin that has been converted by evolution to be used to wave and wiggle and act as an attractant to other hungry fish looking for food; of course, once in range, they soon become the anglerfish's meal. Not all anglerfish are deep-sea monsters – it is a fairly large order of 200 species containing eighteen families (though there is still some ongoing debate over the details of anglerfish taxonomy). The group's names themselves betray the bizarre nature of the species it holds: handfish, seadevils, coffinfish, sea toads dreamers. Probably the most well known (although few realize they are an off-puttingly ugly anglerfish) is the monkfish, the tail of which is occasionally eaten in fancier restaurants.

Bacterial assistance

Only deep-sea anglerfish have the famous 'light-up' or bioluminescent lures, though, and our fanfin angler is no exception – it needed such adaptations, as it lives in the twilight zone of the ocean, between 100–1,510 m (328–4,954 ft) in depth. Known as an esca, this lure – grown at the end of an adapted dorsal fin spine – has the amazing ability to light up like a torch, creating a 'hi-vis' fish. Bioluminescence is a trait that many animals have evolved, and we're discovering more all the time. As well as numerous fish (see also the lanternfish, pages 52–5), various marine life forms such as bacteria, algae, jellyfish, worms, crustaceans, starfish, molluscs and even some sharks have developed the ability – and that's not to mention the terrestrial species of fireflies, click

beetles, flies, centipedes, millipedes, the land snail and various annelid worms, among others, all of which also have this adaptation.

In the case of anglerfish, it isn't the animal that generates bioluminescence. Instead, their escas are specially evolved homes to a kind of photobacterium (that is, a bacterium species that produces light), which lives symbiotically inside the fish. In true symbiotic relationships, there is a mutual benefit for all the creatures involved – in this case, the bacterium gets protection while the fish gets to wave the bacteria around in the gloom to get a meal. The fish do not possess the chemicals to make light themselves (unlike our fabulous lanternfish) and, while juvenile anglerfish don't seem to possess any bacteria until they are adults, the source of this bacteria remains a mystery. Even more confusing or intriguing is the fact that each species of deep-sea anglerfish has its own different type of bacteria. One has to ask: did the micro-organisms evolve with the fish or do they just obtain their bioluminescent bacteria from a different source in their chosen environments?

This is a fish with a face only a mother could love. It's hard to gauge the spread of those strange filamentous fins without a photograph.

Pocket-sized mating

One thing we have discovered, though, is how fanfin anglerfish mate. In the early days of trawling the deep ocean for discoveries – long before submarines and ROVs opened up a window into this mysterious pitch-black world – deep-sea anglerfish were quite frequently brought to the surface in nets; when these fish were examined, they all appeared to be female. Initially, it was thought that the species perhaps bred asexually or that the males might spend most of their time in different areas of the ocean.

Finally, a large female was dredged up from the deep and was found to have a small parasitic fish attached to her side. This was, in fact, a male of the same species that was a fraction of the size of the female. This was truly one of the most startling examples of sexual dimorphism on the planet (which is when males and females of the same species look entirely different). The male was one-tenth of the size of its mate. Krøyer's deep sea anglerfish (*Ceratius hoboelli*) is a much larger species from the same family which can grow to 91 cm (3 ft) in length and has the distinction of having females that are sixty times larger than its males – and nearly half a million times heavier!

The anglerfish male's existence has become entirely centred around finding a female and mating with her. This is not merely because he needs to breed but also because he relies on his association with her to live. Larval males that fail to track down a female within a month inevitably die. How they set about this task is with big eyes and an extremely fine olfactory sense. The males track down the females using smell, though it is unknown whether the females leave a pheromone trail. Once the males find a female, they cling on for dear life – literally. Using a set of jaws that look more like a pair of pliers, they burrow through her skin and tissues using tiny rows of very small teeth. Once they are truly dug in, they fuse with her, eventually becoming a permanent appendage as they are carried around, trailing from her side. The males have no other way of obtaining sustenance, so they gradually connect to her bloodstream, although no one knows exactly how. Ultimately, the male leads a parasitic lifestyle, but it is also useful as it is now in a convenient position to be able to fertilize the eggs when the female is ready to lay (again the hormonal process involved in this is still unknown). However, if you wanted proof that evolution doesn't conform to what we might view as logic, you could do worse than look at the fanfin anglerfish.

Once the males find a female, they cling on for dear life – literally.

28

BURBOT

{Lota lota}

A.K.A.

Mariah, freshwater cod, 'the lawyer'

SIZE

Around 40 cm (16 in)

HABITAT

Deep, cold rivers and lakes

DISTINGUISHING FEATURES

A giant tadpole with sharp teeth

PERSONALITY

Secretive and slimy

LIKES

The cold

SPECIAL SKILLS

Lays millions of eggs

CONSERVATION STATUS

Least Concern

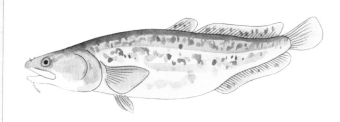

A FISH OF MANY names – which also include mariah, freshwater cod, 'the lawyer', coneyfish and eelpout – burbot has the kind of face only their mothers could love, with a strange fleshy projection or barbel on its lower lip. The name 'burbot' derives from the Latin *barba* meaning 'beard', and even the fish's scientific name *Lota* is also a translation – this time from the Old French name *lotte*, referring to the same well-known species of fish. The old-fashioned name, eelpout, probably derives from a resemblance to an eel (with a dash of catfish), while 'the lawyer' is also believed to refer to the fish's 'beard'.

Ice-cold lawyer

Burbot is an Ice Age relic that is likely to have once dominated most of the continent's freshwater habitats while in the frozen grip of glaciation over the last few million years (technically we are still in the same period, though the effects of global warming may seem to belie this fact). This is a species well adapted to the cold. It is found right across the Holarctic (the global far north), from France through all of Europe and into Siberia, as well as Alaska right across to New Brunswick, Canada. They are common and well known in Lake Erie and the rest of the Great Lakes. The fish was even found in Britain until 1969 when it was finally wiped out by agricultural chemical run-off and heavy-metal pollution.

Burbot is the only freshwater species of the cod order. Consequently, if you wanted to find its closest relatives, you would have to trawl the North Sea for Atlantic cod, haddock, whiting and pollock – those notoriously overfished food species that live in the cold depths towards Arctic seas.

The British have somewhat of a love–hate relationship with burbot – at one point, they were so common in Britain that they were fed to pigs. Despite this dishonour, the species is so delicious that it is generally considered a delicacy in many countries even to this day. It is sometimes called 'the poor man's lobster' owing to its sweet flesh, tasting similar to that popular and expensive crustacean. As they are now extinct in the UK, burbot is a clear favourite for the reintroduction programmes that have been so successful with our Ice Age and medieval mammal and birds – and the current vogue for 'rewilding' should soon help this happen. Both Germany and Belgium have successfully boosted their dwindling burbot numbers already, indicating possible success in any mooted British reintroduction scheme.

Burbot has the kind of face only their mothers could love.

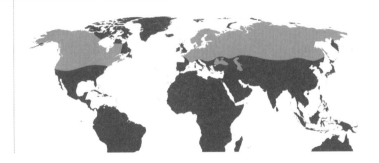

Cod almighty

Burbot is frequently the apex predator in its home territories. It may not look like much – and northern pike (see pages 22–5) often live in the same lakes, reciprocally eating burbot fry as burbot eat young pike – but removing or losing top predators from such closed ecosystems can have catastrophic local and national impacts, even if we are slow to notice. Despite fears – from anglers especially – that rewilded burbot will eat young gamefish, as well as sticklebacks and minnows, the addition of a formerly naturally occurring top predator will more likely restore the well-maintained ecological balance in the long run.

One female Burbot can lay as many as 3 million eggs.

Of course, larger-scale landscape changes than fisheries and lakes are more damaging to the burbot's chances. In many places in North America, hydroelectric dams have been built to provide power for large conurbations – but also inadvertently damming up the migration and dispersal routes for many fish species, preventing them from colonizing new areas and breeding; for the fish, including burbot, this has been like building the Berlin Wall across an autobahn or highway. Like a lot of other freshwater fish, burbot prefer to migrate to their spawning grounds and, once deprived of their traditional routes, cannot breed. One female burbot can lay as many as 3 million eggs, which explains how common the species once was, but the lower modern numbers of burbot become very finite sometimes, leading to population collapse within a single generation. Burbot, despite its reputedly delicious flavour, doesn't rate highly as a commercial fish, and so it is not afforded much in the way of protection. Although once upon a time that was not the case at all.

Historically, the fish was responsible for a massive commercial success story. Ted and Joseph Rowell were fur farmers back in the 1930s in Minnesota. At the time, burbot was cheap and plentiful and available locally and the furriers began to feed their captive foxes with the fish. To their surprise, these blue foxes' coats became known as being the best in the country.

Fine, fine fox fur

This newly renowned superiority got the Rowells thinking. Ted, who was a pharmacist by trade, started wondering if there was something in the 'eelpouts' they were using as fox food that might have had such a desirable effect on the foxes' fur. He discovered burbot oil, a natural oil every self-effacing burbot produces to combat the cold and which contains more than four times the vitamin D and as much as ten times the vitamin A as traditional cod liver oil; not only that, but the fish make lots of this oil. The Rowells sent a sample of burbot oil off to a laboratory for assaying and the results that came back were astonishing: the fish's livers, where the oil is made, can make up 10 per cent of their body weight, while human livers make up less than 2 per cent, and it was likely to be this oil that enhanced the quality of the foxes' fur and so impressed their customers.

The Rowells were inspired to set up a new business called the Burbot Liver Products Company (nowadays part of Solvay Pharmaceuticals, based in Brussels, Belgium) that went on to make the family business a small fortune – especially when the Second World War began and cod liver oil exports were closed down. However, there's nothing new under the sun, and it emerged that burbot livers were a sought-after delicacy in France hundreds of year ago by the ladies of the era, in all likelihood for the same reason: it was good for their hair and skin.

Burbot are tough. They are born into the cold. The burbot breeding season is early winter to early spring, so they often spawn under the ice. But this habit of moving around even in the deepest winter must surely have given our ancestors the difference between survival and starvation in the colder parts of the world, when nature has locked away almost anything nutritious. We owe them a debt of gratitude, although I suspect we shall continue to overlook the appeal or the importance of these peculiar fish.

These are fish that really love the cold.

29

GREAT HAMMERHEAD

{*Sphyrna mokarran*}

A.K.A.

Squat-headed hammer, *jarjur* (Arabic)

SIZE

Up to 6 m (20 ft)

HABITAT

Tropical waters

DISTINGUISHING FEATURES

Head is a hammer

PERSONALITY

Solitary

LIKES

Stingrays

SPECIAL SKILLS

Rolling motion

CONSERVATION STATUS

Critically Endangered

A WIDE-RANGING TOUR OF the world's oceans will reveal a veritable tool kit attached to the heads of several different kinds of fish. The aquatic handyman will have access to a blade in the form of a swordfish (see striped marlin, pages 14–17), a saw via the front end of a sawfish and – perhaps strangest of all – a hammer in the shape of the head of a shark species. While humans only invented the hammer as a tool relatively recently, this odd family of sharks has had its mallet-shaped head for more than 200 million years. As to what the purpose of that hammer is – well, this is a question that many marine biologists have been pondering for a long time. The trouble is that there are four seemingly good

The purpose of that hammer is a question that many marine biologists have been pondering.

answers, but perhaps only one is likely to be correct.

There are nine species in the Sphyrnidae family and all of their English names take that famous head shape into account. The winghead shark (*Eusphyra blochii*) is now my new favourite because its abnormal head can be as much as 50 per cent the size of its body. The smooth hammer (*S. zygaena*) – sounding very much like a tool selection in a DIY shop – is the second biggest, followed by the scalloped hammerhead (*S. lewini*), which are the ones that shoal in the huge numbers sometimes seen on TV natural history programmes. Large shoals are now getting much harder to see as this species is one of the worst-hit by the illicit trade in shark fins. These hammerheads are the only sharks that tend to form shoals during the day, though they can become solitary hunters at night. The scalloped bonnethead, the scoophead, the bonnethead, the smalleye hammerhead and the recently discovered Carolina hammerhead all have – as well as their engagingly illustrative names – a cephalofoil, the technical name for what is objectively an amazingly shaped head.

Under the hammer

With all these species managing to sustain and diverge with that head shape, it clearly serves an important evolutionary purpose – but what is it? Some ichthyologists believe it evolved for the sharks to swim more efficiently. The hydrofoil face reduces the drag of the water and

gives the sharks lift when they are swimming along. Put simply, this means they are more efficient in the water, expending less energy when mobile. Great hammerheads have been observed swimming on their sides in a sort of rolling motion which, due to their large dorsal and pectoral fins, means they can cruise at good speeds with a minimum of effort.

Their mouths always seem out of proportion with the size of their heads.

The second theory is that their heads evolved to enable them to hunt fish buried in the sand. Great hammerheads particularly favour stingrays; we know this because many hammerheads have been seen with the rays' stingers stuck in their faces as leftovers from a tasty, if rather painful, meal. There is also evidence the sharks might be mostly immune to the effects of the ray toxins. As hammerheads swim over the sand, they can be seen turning their heads from side to side, as if searching for a signal, like metal detectorists looking for Roman coins. If a faint signal is detected by the plentiful electroreceptors on the sharks' heads, they can triangulate the signal, pinpoint their prey and grab it while catching it unawares.

The third hypothesis is that the hammerheads evolved to be able to see better. This is a rather new theory and might seem a little counter-intuitive when you regard those small eyes placed out on stalks to form the 'hammer'. Hammerheads were always thought to have monocular vision because of the placement of their eyes, but research has shown that they have good binocular vision – in fact, some of the best among sharks. This allows them to see while hunting prey and gives them great depth perception, which is especially useful when hunting fast-swimming and manoeuvring stingrays.

The fourth and last theory is that they evolved those amazing heads to help them hold their prey down to eat it safely. There are some reports of hammerheads pinning down stingrays while biting off their wings to make them easier to consume and less likely to escape. Great hammerheads are specialists in eating their own kind, which includes other sharks and rays from the same few orders of cartilaginous fish. You could say it takes a shark to catch a shark.

From sledgehammer to mallet

The solution to this quandary came, perhaps surprisingly, from the field of DNA analysis. Led by Professor Andrew Martin, a team from Colorado University, based in Boulder, revealed that one of the more counter-intuitive suggestions might be true. Many biologists believed that the hammer trait had probably started off small, with an ancestor that looked like the bonnet shark evolving to have larger and more extreme head shapes as the benefits of this feature gave its owner an advantage. But actually, the ancestral form had a massive head, making my new favourite the winghead shark, the most like the original hammerhead. They started with large heads and subsequently evolved smaller heads in different environments.

Research has shown that they have good binocular vision.

But which of our theories is correct? The truth is that all four are all likely to contribute to the success of the hammerhead group, which is to be found in all the coastal and continental shelf waters between the temperate zones and southern oceans. Marine biologists will continue to investigate in forensic detail to find out exactly why the hammerheads have such remarkable heads.

— Chapter 5 —

PUSHING THE EXTREMES

Fish are masters of the extreme. Found in almost every water-based habitat on Earth (and occasionally not even in water) – from the steaming hot to the freezing cold, from shallow riverbeds to the crushing and pitch-black deep – fish forms and lives can undergo incredible evolutionary transformations, making them the supreme masters of camouflage and lords of every biome they inhabit. The following collection of wonders demonstrates ably that fish are prone to break out from anything that could be called 'normal' and push the limits of what is possible – and by doing so, they could well teach us new and enlightening things that might change all our perceptions for good.

30 | BLACKFIN ICEFISH

{Chaenocephalus aceratus}

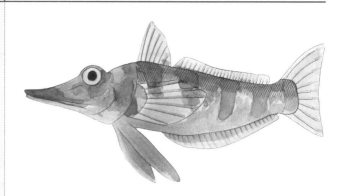

Though it sounds like a baddie in a James Bond film, the blackfin or crocodile icefish is as harmless as a fish could be, in reality. However, getting to see one is a dangerous endeavour. There are at least sixteen species that go by the name of 'crocodile icefish' and all live and thrive only in the Southern Ocean. This is the great hemispherical ocean that surrounds Antarctica and has the distinction of being constantly the coldest water in the world. Temperatures there can reach −1.8°C (28.8°F), cold enough to easily freeze the blood in human veins – though we would remain conscious for less than 15 minutes and be dead within 45 minutes even in water at 0°C (32°F). Clearly, these fish must have a host of special adaptations to live where they do – so what are they?

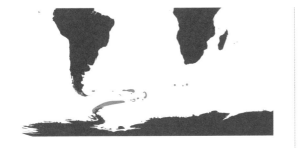

Clearly, these fish must have a host of special adaptations to live where they do.

Thawing the blood

A good way of surviving the intense cold is to pump your body full of antifreeze. This isn't the same kind of antifreeze we put into our car engines, but it essentially does the same thing: it lowers the freezing temperature of the water in the fish. Icefish have a natural antifreeze which is composed of a glycol-protein that attaches to ice crystals as they form in the blood and prevents them from growing. This means the crystals can't fuse and are unable to freeze the blood solid. Cold water removes the heat from our bodies thirty times faster than cold air, so icefish need all the protection against the cold they can muster when living off the coastal shelf of the Antarctic continent. Icefish truly have their survival strategy worked out.

Their adaptations stretch well beyond antifreeze; icefish evolution has removed all extraneous physical attributes that aren't needed for survival in freezing seawater. Their low-density bones are extremely light so they can swim with very little effort; they have an extremely slow metabolism, only needing to eat sparingly (though when they do, they can consume a very large meal with their preposterously big, crocodile-like jaws); and they generally avoid interactions with any rival species. Icefish are also the only vertebrates on Earth without haemoglobin (that is, red blood cells) in their blood. So they are highly anaemic and have white blood one might expect in an alien life form. Every other vertebrate needs blood to transport oxygen around its body, so how does this unique condition work?

Oxygen-free fish?

There has been quite a lot of scientific work on this subject now – partly because, if it makes icefish able to live in near-freezing conditions, then perhaps we can gain a deeper understanding and reap the benefits suggested by the secrets of a blood-free life. What has been discovered is incredibly complicated and I hope that I'm able to explain it now. Blood is mainly composed of two substances. It is around 55 per cent plasma, which is a liquid containing water, ions, minerals, nutrients and a surprising amount of waste materials moving around in it. The rest is made up of three kinds of cell: red blood cells, which makes our blood red and contains the haemoglobin proteins necessary to bind with oxygen and carry it around our bodies; white blood cells, which are a major weapon in our immune systems; and platelets, which cause the congealing that stops us from bleeding out.

A fish without haemoglobin still must transport oxygen to its organs and around its body – but how? It turns out that icefish transport oxygen through their plasma. This is not nearly as efficient at oxygen transportation as haemoglobin, which means that the fish

The icefish might be seen as one of very few of evolutionary experiments that 'went wrong'.

have had to evolve much larger hearts to pump around the relatively huge volumes of plasma they need to move. They also have enlarged blood vessels to carry these greater volumes around the body – just so they can get enough to live and function. Even the muscles in their hearts are spongy – heart muscles being notoriously oxygen-hungry organs – so that they can absorb oxygen directly from the plasma as it passes through.

All of which is fine and amazing, but where is the advantage to not having any red blood? There doesn't appear to be any. Nothing in nature occurs by accident; everything has been driven by some greater pressure, and we just have to find it. The only answer that scientists have come up with is vague at best.

No competition

What we do know, now that its entire genome has been mapped out, is that the blackfin icefish evolved more than 77 million years ago. It has a common ancestor with another entrant in this book: the three-spined stickleback (see pages 48–51). At that time in the planet's history (known as the Campanian Era of the Late Cretaceous period, when tyrannosaurs were wandering the terrestrial earth), the Earth' sea level was much higher than it is today. North America was in pieces and Antarctica was still travelling to the bottom of the world and didn't settle into its present position until 40 million years ago. As Antarctica headed south, some weird little fish went along with it.

For reasons as yet unknown, ecological competition – one of the great drivers of evolution – fell away. As the sea got colder the further south the continent moved, this lack of competition enabled – somehow – a fish with no haemoglobin to appear, survive and continue to breed. Even though there was no real benefit to being without haemoglobin, at the time it didn't hinder the icefish either – there was nothing else around that had haemoglobin to compete with it and do a better job and so the bloodless icefish was born.

This is one of the hardest fish on the planet to see – unless you are an Antarctic scuba diver.

What can we learn from this amazing fish's myriad adaptations? The answer seems to be very little, other than we need red blood to survive. The icefish might be seen as one of very few of nature's evolutionary experiments that 'went wrong' in a way, but the fish somehow survived – which is remarkable enough in itself.

31

MEXICAN TETRA

{Astyanax mexicanus}

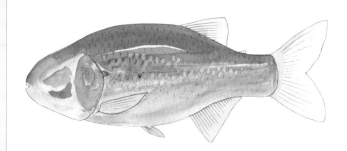

THE MEXICAN TETRA is a small, greenish fish with two obvious very big and distinct eyes on the side of its head. It is an attractive and popular aquarium species found in the wild in the warm waters of the Nueces and Pecos rivers in Mexico, and up into the USA, via the Rio Grande river to Texas. They school in large numbers and could be described as common.

What makes the tetra truly extraordinary is that it also has a colourless (well, pinkish) and blind underground form that lives entirely in caves. Genetically the two forms are identical – they are the same species.

A Jekyll and Hyde character

How did this happen? Like Dr Jekyll and Mr Hyde, is this a fish with a monster hiding inside? Or is it a remarkably adapted species to take full advantage of all the opportunities in the large and wide-ranging ecosystem of the Sierra del Abra caves? This system includes some thirty major caves, each of which has these fish living in them. The caves have intriguing names, such as Molino, Los Sabinos, Yerbaniz and Cueva Chica; this last is the location where the blind form was first discovered in 1936 and where all aquarium individuals originated from. All these caves demand professional caving equipment to access and each holds a mix of surface forms with eyesight fish, intermediate forms and the blind cave fish.

So why go blind? Blind cave fish are one of the best and most studied examples of evolution at work. The species' schizophrenic evolution has been driven by the pressures to be faster, see better, to carve out its own space from other fish and to derive enough energy to keep the whole engine running. When those pressures change, evolution can get very creative indeed.

As the Mexican tetra's blind form lives in complete darkness all its life, it does not need to develop eyes that need light to see with. Creating and growing eyes with neurones, retinas and lenses, as well as relaying information back to the brain, all takes a lot of energy. The fish can survive without sight in its light-free environment – thus saving a large part of its daily energy requirement.

As a consequence of saving energy on the processing of visual information, the blind cave fish also has a reduced brain size compared to its daylight-living relatives of a similar size. A large brain in itself needs energy to run and maintain, so reducing its size conserves its energy reserves by default. According to a recent study, Mexican tetras use 23 per cent of their brain capacity for processing, while blind cave

The Mexican tetra can survive without sight in its light-free environment.

fish only use 10 per cent. What this tells us is that caves are good places to live, having few predators, but this lifestyle comes at a heavy cost. Finding enough food to survive is not so easy, particularly in a lightless cave. If a fish does without a large, demanding engine, it doesn't need as much fuel and stands a better chance of surviving. This theory is known as the expensive-tissue theory and makes particular sense in the almost alien world of the blind cave fish.

Sensory deprivation

Blind cave fish have even more adaptations to their natural sensory-deprivation tanks. It has now been discovered that they barely sleep, are never full of food and have blood-sugar levels that would kill the average human – yet they remain healthy and appropriately active. Studies of this form are being used to help us understand diabetes and autism. All from a fish that never sees the light of day!

The blind cave fish only sleeps for less than two hours a day at any one time on average (their surface brethren get six hours every day). Due to the paucity of food in their limited environments, if a prey item suddenly appears, the fish cannot miss out. It also lacks the circadian rhythms or internal body clock that almost all other animals and plants possess in some form. Even humans have circadian rhythms – that's why we often roughly know what time it is even when we're deprived of daylight. Running these internal body clocks is so important that a lot of energy is given over to it in our bodies to enable us to judge the time of day. The blind cave fish has lost this ability in its unchanging world of eternal night.

Then there is the eating. The blind cave fish lacks the gene that tells its body that it's 'full.' In addition, it can store up to four times more fat in its body than its surface-dwelling relatives. On occasion, some humans lack this gene, with disastrous effects: the feeling of being full is our bodies' way of not overdosing on food that we can't process. Blind cave fish, however, never have this feeling. The high sugar levels of the species are also incredibly dangerous in humans and other animals and are naturally maintained at a lower level by the insulin hormone produced in the pancreas gland to help control those levels. Without insulin, our cells cannot absorb the glucose sugar they need, preventing them from working properly. It is well known that an inability to produce enough insulin causes diabetes. The blind cave fish does not even have any insulin but, despite this, its cells work fine. If we can discover how, then we could well go a step closer to making millions of people's lives much, much better.

The blind cave fish does not even have any insulin.

When you live in a cave and are never quite sure when your next meal is going to wash or drop in, dietary pragmatism is often necessary. For example, blind cave fish have been found to include bat droppings as a major part of their diet. Once a source of food has been discovered, it must be made the most of. Blind cave fish must remain awake, on the edge of hunger and catholic in their tastes – devoting time and energy to maintaining low blood sugar levels would be a complete waste of time. All of these adaptations are also present in their surface relatives but unused. This is where it gets exciting.

Biologists hope that, by studying these strange 'alternate' fish, they might discover more fully the genetic processes responsible, allow us to find similar traits in humans – and then save millions of lives.

32

AROWANA

{Osteoglossum bicirrhosum}

A.K.A.

Dragonfish, water
monkeys

SIZE

Up to 90 cm (35 in)

HABITAT

Tropical waters

**DISTINGUISHING
FEATURES**

Moustached snake

PERSONALITY

Entrepreneurial

LIKES

Feeding at night

SPECIAL SKILLS

Can leap 2 m (6 ft 7 in)
out of the water

**CONSERVATION
STATUS**

Endangered

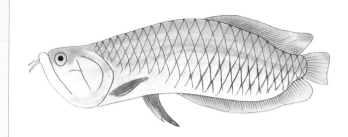

T HE LITTLE TICKLE on the surface of the water – like
an invisible person is drawing patterns there – that's
what gives this species away. The arowana are a successful
modern fish group born in the late Jurassic period (about
163.5–145 million years ago) when most of the Earth's
land was joined together in a huge 'supercontinent'
known as Gondwanaland. Osteoglossids have nine
representative species spread across the tropical regions
of the globe in South America, Africa, Asia and Australia.
All are very easy to recognize with those natty little
moustaches and sinuous, almost snake-like, bodies. The
scientific family name Osteoglossidae translates as 'bony
tongues', from the Latin *osteo* for bone and *glossum* for
tongue. This is very appropriate despite its odd sound:
inside arowana mouths are bony tongues encrusted with
teeth, which they use to crush their prey. Arowana are
hunters – those cavernous mouths are designed for one
thing only: to snatch food.

Inside arowana mouths are bony tongues encrusted with teeth.

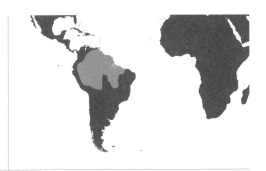

Amazonian superpower

Arowana don't just take prey from the water – they have a remarkable superpower that enables them to hunt food out of the water, too. In South America, arowana live in the Amazon River. Every year, around the same time, it starts to rain continuously and their home quickly trebles in size. The waters are no longer confined by the banks, and the water breaks out, flooding the surrounding rainforest – so that underwater world not only increases in size but also becomes a sunken garden. This creates new opportunities for the more entrepreneurial fish species; in the case of arowana, those opportunities can be found dangling from the low branches of the now-flooded forest: arboreal spiders, beetles and insects are all now within range of what are the high-jump champions of the piscean world.

Arowana can leap as much as 2 m (6 ft 7 in) out of the water from a floating, suspended start to pull a precarious meal off its perch; they have even been found with birds and bats in their stomachs on occasion! This leap is a huge twice as high as they are long (really big arowana can measure up to one metre in length). To put that into human terms, Cuban athlete Javier Sotomayor jumped a staggering 2.45 m (8 ft) high in Salamanca, Spain, in 1993 – a world record. He stands at 195 cm (6 ft 4 in) and to compete with an arowana, he would have had to jump 3.9 m (12 ft 8 in).

Arowana are able to jump this high owing to that sinuous body. They curl themselves into an almost perfect 'S' shape, arch their backs, spread out their wide pectoral fins and flatten their tails. They then push up, straightening their muscles and leap, like a rocket from a silo. This ability to leap clear of the water has given them the rather amusing but descriptive nickname of 'water monkeys' in South America.

Prehistoric elegance

Arowana have an elegant appearance that appeals to the worldwide aquarium trade – although a firm lid is recommended for their tanks – aquarists go quite mad for them. In 2009, it was reported that a fully grown albino super red arowana (*Scleropages legendrei*) from Indonesia was sold for $300,000 to a Chinese official. There are 150 CITES (Convention for the International Trade for Endangered Species, which monitors and protects endangered and threatened species) registered arowana fish farms across Singapore, Malaysia and Indonesia. The fish are chipped and DNA-tagged to prevent theft. A small arowana can sell for $2,000. There is even a fish plastic surgeon that can make your arowana more beautiful if necessary. With so much money involved, there is an unscrupulous underworld of subterfuge and intrigue surrounding arowana collecting and dealing – so much so, that the trade since 2012 had an estimated value of around $200 million.

Even a small arowana can sell for $2,000.

The fish at the centre of all of this madness is the Asian arowana (*S. formosus*), a fish that is so endangered that it is one of only eight freshwater fish in Appendix I of the CITES list, which entitles it to the strictest legislation there is (along with rhinoceros horn and elephant ivory). Wild Asian arowana are found throughout South-east Asia in different haplotypes (halotypes means distinctive-looking forms that are considered the same species). Green arowana are the most common and are found throughout Indonesia; silver Asian arowana are found in Borneo; red-tailed golden arowana in Sumatra; Bukit Merah blue in Peninsular Malaysia; and, lastly, the super red arowana, found only in a couple of rivers in Borneo.

The red wild form is only found in Southeast Asia.

Beyond the madness

All of these varied forms live in river systems that have suffered severely from habitat degradation caused mostly by the palm oil trade, which has seen huge swathes of rainforest destroyed, decimating the water table and natural river systems. Arowana are also slow breeders, only reaching sexual maturity at around 3–4 years old (very old for most fish species) and only laying between thirty and sixty eggs. Male arowana look after the eggs and young in their large mouths). Green arowana and its closely related forms are under immense pressure.

The aquarium trade, even if willing, is unable to help in the fish's plight. While arowana readily breed in captivity, there is no habitat to release them back into. Many of the captive arowana breeders have another obsession to go along with the coveting and enhancing of the fish's natural beauty: crossbreeding the different haplotypes to create hybrids of varying colours. The most sought-after is 'Gold and Red', although albinos obviously demand high prices, too.

In China, Asian arowana forms are known as 'dragonfish' – and with those large, reflective scales, small barbels and serpentine movements, it's easy to see why. Keeping arowana is also seen as good feng shui, balancing yang (wind 'energy') with yin (water 'energy'). This means that arowana become very prized and revered possessions of their owners – there is even a legend that the fish will leap to its death, sacrificing its own life so that its owner might live.

33

DEVILS HOLE
PUPFISH

{*Cyprinodon diabolis*}

*Pupfish are so-called because they
have the delightful reputation of
being quite playful.*

THERE ARE ONLY a handful of creatures able to live
in the hottest habitat on Earth – and one of them
happens to be a fish. Death Valley, Nevada, USA – only
209 km (130 miles) from Las Vegas – has the honour
of holding the record of the highest temperature ever
recorded. On 10 July 1913, a temperature of 56.7°C
(134°F) was logged in the aptly named Furnace
Creek. This is the lowest place on the North American

continent, well below sea level and almost rain-free, due to its position between mountain ranges – an unlikely place to find a fish. However, in a permanent waterhole in the form of an underwater aquifer known as the Devils Hole, you will find the Devils Hole pupfish.

Playful pupfish

Pupfish are so-called because they have the delightful reputation of being quite playful – like puppies, although this seemingly adorable behaviour is the males fighting rather than playing. There are 120 species of pupfish known to science, but the Devils Hole pupfish are rather different to the others, despite sharing a genus with many of them: they have reduced pelvic fins, are much smaller in size and do not breed as often. These features are most likely all adaptations to living in isolation in the desert long enough to have evolved into an entirely separate species – but the real mystery is how they got into this small and remote waterhole in the first place.

Previously, biologists have thought the species to have been in situ for somewhere between 10,000–20,000 years, suggesting that its ancestors might have got trapped there as the world around them changed. Tectonic activity around that time lowered the Nevada plate, changing major watercourses as well as pushing temperatures up and lowering rainfall. This would have left any population of small, blue fish permanently trapped in their 500-m- (1,650-ft-) deep sinkhole in the middle of a desert. However, more recently, the pupfish have had their genome mapped against their closest living relative, found just a few miles away – the Death Valley pupfish (*C. salinus*) and discovered that the two species had only been separated for around 1,000 years. The desert was then already uncrossable for a fish, leaving just two other logical methods for the fish's arrival – accidental transport by humans or birds. A likely scenario is this: fish eggs are tiny and sticky, so if they got attached to an animal at one waterhole they might well wash off at the next (particularly if they've lost a little stickiness by slightly drying out); this would mean that at least one fish was able to migrate to its new home. Over many years, this may well have happened more than once. While this story remains hypothetical, it's the best we have come up with – but the exact method remains a mystery.

A natural aquarium

It's a small location for a full species to develop, for sure: only a few metres wide, with an average water temperature of 92°C (198°F), almost boiling, and a depth of 500 m (1,640 ft), although no one has plumbed the bottom. There is only a tiny rock ledge under the water where algae can grow, and the sun only gets to it for a few minutes a day – just enough for it to photosynthesize. This has become the pupfish's sole buffet table and also the only site where they can breed and safely hide their eggs. This is truly a miracle in tenacity. In fact, Devils Hole pupfish has the smallest geographic range of any known vertebrate on Earth. In a place where high temperatures, low levels of dissolved oxygen and very limited food resources are standard, this

Devils Hole is a bizarre and unique ecosystem.

is about as tenuous a grasp on a life as can be imagined. Add to this the fact that the fish only inhabit the top 80 m (262 ft) – the only region of the sinkhole where sunlight and oxygen levels make life sustainable. Devils Hole also undergoes the occasional catastrophic event, when it seethes like a geyser due to seismic activity in places as far away as Japan or Indonesia, for reasons yet unknown.

To many living in the United States, the fish are treated like ecological superstars. Forever extremely endangered by default, the American people have taken the species to heart. Perhaps they represent a triumph of the American spirit, success in permanent adversity – and theirs is a heroic ongoing story, for sure. The Devils Hole pupfish also has the status of being the first species in the States to have resulted in a man being successfully prosecuted for killing one and sentenced to twelve months in prison.

One of the most protected fish on the planet.

Desert fragility

This pupfish lives such a fragile life that scientists constantly monitor them with on-site cameras for any irregularities (that is exactly how the hapless drunk man that went for a swim was caught and sent to jail). Every year, these biological guardians climb into the hot bath-like water and undertake a population census of the fish. In 1995, that number was a healthy 200 in spring, rising to 300–500 after a good breeding season; winter populations take a hit even in this permanently hot desert, probably due to lack of food. However, everyone got a fright in 2006 when the census logged no more than thirty-five individuals. It would take very little to wipe this species off the face of the planet – a cloudy day or a heatwave could do this, so everyone panicked. Cooler heads set up a breeding programme, keeping some of the surviving Devils Hole pupfish off-site in a laboratory so that if it ever did fully disappear there would be an 'insurance' population to replace them.

Today, the situation is much more reassuring, with the 2019 survey registering a return to former levels with 136 individuals present. In the meantime, biologists are continuing to find out what happened to reduce the population so drastically. Devils Hole is a bizarre and unique ecosystem and it may never be known why the fish that plays like a puppy almost became extinct overnight, but it's a boost for the American spirit and fish-lovers everywhere that it lingers on.

34

GREAT BLUE-SPOTTED MUDSKIPPER

{Boleophthalmus pectinirostris}

WHILE MOST FISH are notoriously water-loving, there is one subfamily of the gobies (family Oxudercidae) which spends about 90 per cent of its time living on land. Admittedly, they live on mud mostly but also look very striking with their unusual movements, bug eyes and – to us – comically downturned mouths. They have also evolved to break their piscean programming and fill a niche in nature usually only exploited by crabs, snails and mud worms: the intertidal world that appears twice a day for several hours, before being submerged in the sea once more. To conquer this eternally changing world of mud has taken a specific kind of tenacity – a hardiness that belongs to the thirty-two species of fish known as the mudskippers (subfamily Oxudercinae).

Mudskippers can absorb oxygen from the surrounding air through their skin.

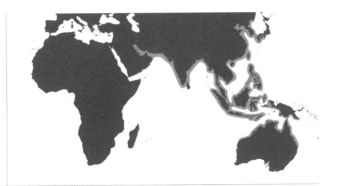

Fish take to the land

The evolutionary history of all terrestrial vertebrate life began when primitive fish first took to the land on their way to becoming amphibians, then reptiles, birds and mammals. By studying the lowly mudskipper, we can go some way to solving the great mystery of how this is most likely to have happened.

Before any fish can climb out on to land and live there comfortably, three major physiological issues need to be addressed: How do I breathe? How do I move? How do I stay alive – that is, eat, mate and stay away from danger? All of these problems have been solved by mudskippers in their indomitable way.

When a mudskipper emerges on to the land, it gulps down water retained in its gills – rather like the air in scuba tanks. This gives it a ready oxygen supply when it is needed. However, it has also evolved another trick – one seen in frogs and other amphibians: mudskippers can absorb oxygen from the surrounding air through their skin. The skin has to remain moist and is the most likely key to understanding how gills might have been dispensed within the deep mists of time, as they became water tanks, before being lost entirely and swapped for breathing through the skin. Termed cutaneous respiration, mudskippers can use this technique to continue to slow down the loss of water from their gills and even breathe for a short while after it has run out. Their skin can even sense when it is dehydrating, telling

the fish to head back to their burrows, which are always filled with water; a quick dip and roll and the fish are good to go once more – plus, remember that the tide is never too far away, so any danger of suffocation is always temporary.

They share the mudflats with worms and crabs.

Fins become legs

Water is very good at supporting an animal's body, and this support needs to be substituted for somehow when mudskippers move on to the land. This is done with the help of exceedingly strong pectoral fins on the sides of their bodies. The fins are muscular and can be rotated almost like clockwork toys to propel themselves along the surface of the soft mud. The pelvic fins on the underside have also evolved into two tiny gripping 'hands', allowing the fish to hold on to surfaces with its 'suckers'. This ability also allows mudskippers to climb near-vertical surfaces such as mangrove roots and the slimy rocks of even very high waterfalls.

General survival presents a set of somewhat different issues. Even so, mudskippers have come up with some clever solutions – particularly with regard to their eyes. If you put your head underwater without goggles, you'll be aware that seeing underwater, although not impossible, is significantly different from seeing through the air. Mudskippers can do both, in such a way that biologists are now studying their eyes to discover new clues about how life evolved to live on land.

Mudskippers also have a surprisingly strong immune system. Using the land for foraging and breeding gives a whole new set of problems to face from a bacteriological and virological point of view. A problem these little fish have again solved. We are only just beginning to explore mudskippers' immunological secrets.

Mudskippers make out

Out on the mudflats, mudskipper mating is also novel. Getting spotted by a prospective sexual partner is very difficult in such a flat world. So the male great blue-spotted mudskipper has developed a flamboyance of fins and finery with a startling array of blue spots all up and down its body. If this is not enough, the males have developed a more startling way to get seen: they leap right up into the air. The higher a fish can leap, the stronger and fitter it probably is – and the more likely it is that neighbourhood females will be able to see him. Sound may also be playing a role: recent studies have shown that the slapping sound made by the males landing on the mud could be sending out subsonic messages through the ground, further exciting the females.

Once the females have seen an attractive male and flopped and sidled over (that's how they move!), he takes her down into his bachelor burrow, where they mate. The fertilized eggs are deposited inside the burrow and it is then the male's job to protect them. In the case of the Japanese mudskipper, the eggs are stuck to the walls of the burrow inside an air bubble – so that they are not submerged in water until they are ready to hatch. So, mudskippers spend their first few days of life on planet Earth already accustomed to living out of water. When they do finally emerge and skip out on to the mudflats, they are completely unaware that their family has solved possibly the greatest evolutionary step in natural history.

Mudskipper mating is also novel.

35

SEADRAGON

{Phyllopteryx taeniolatus} / *{Phycodurus eques}*

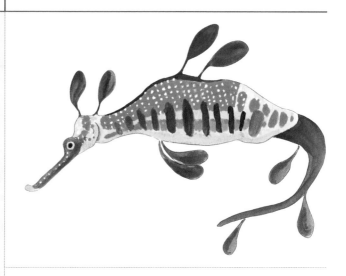

Take a good look at my illustration of a common seadragon – it almost looks as if I have made it up. They do exist and have developed a look as exotic as this, all in the name of camouflage. Perhaps its colours are a little flamboyant to be described as camouflage, but once those extra filaments and flourishes are brought into play, these unique members of the seahorse family can disappear in plain sight – moving almost magically in complete harmony with the seagrasses or seaweeds among which they live. These fish can disappear in front of your very eyes!

All of those seemingly extraneous undulating and waving appendages are more than just extra parts of

Seadragons are the hummingbirds of the ocean.

the fins – some of this ornamentation – most notably the fish's 'horns' – has evolved from its skin, growing out at all angles. They don't aid swimming, however, but are intended to make the fish look a lot less like a fish, and in this purpose, they more than succeed.

Disruptive patterns

Seadragons have 'real' fins to do the swimming: small pectoral fins on the neck, which manage poise and balance, plus a larger dorsal fin used purely for propulsion. These propulsive organs are transparent and near-impossible to see moving, when in fact they are usually working furiously. Seadragons are the hummingbirds of the ocean, flapping their fins at 70 beats per second (hummingbirds usually manage around 80 wingbeats per second). All this effort just to make it look effortless – when the fish is barely moving! The camouflage, the furious hovering and the ornate, vegetation-mimicking fins are all to create the illusion that a seadragon is not real but just a piece of colourful flotsam adrift on the currents.

This disruptive pattern is not a seadragon's only defence. Evolution has also fused all of its scales to create a rugged armour – which is why they hold their shape almost perfectly like little seadragon mummies when they dry out – however, this does mean their bodies are not flexible. They have a pliability that enables them to move more like weeds in the current. There are other members of the pipefish and seahorse family which also specialize in covert operations – the halimeda ghost pipefish of the Indian Ocean, for example, looks exactly like a single leaf – so it's a genuine family trait to be a perfect master of disguise.

However, despite the family's global distribution, you have a very limited set of options if you want to see a seadragon in nature. There are only three species and they are all confined to the southern end of Australia and Tasmania. The common seadragon is globally restricted to the coastal waters of southern Australia, between New South Wales and Geraldton, where it lives on rock reefs and seaweed beds. The leafy seadragon, or 'leafy' as it is affectionately known in Oz, is found from Wilsons Promontory in Victoria in the east to Jurien Bay, north of Perth in the west. Along this stretch of shoreline it haunts kelp beds, seagrass clumps and open stretches of sand. There are a few hot-spot locations, and the Australians have even set up a 'Dragon Search' hotline to report sightings, should you see one. Understanding where seadragons can be found is vitally important to help preserve these uniquely Australian sea creatures. Both species are fully protected by law, so any coastal developments have to jump through legal hoops to make sure the welfare of these guys is one of the first things any stakeholder has to take into consideration.

Seadragons are very sensitive to change.

Hidden gem

Further offshore is found the third species, the ruby seadragon, which inhabits much deeper waters than the other two and which was only discovered in 2015. This deep red species grows to 23 cm (9 in) in length and has more stumpy lobes, rather than the leaf-like protuberances found in the other two.

A seadragon's camouflage does not always mean it remains safe. Recent studies have indicated that the seadragon's complete dependence on seagrass beds, coral and seagrasses for hiding places could be its Achilles heel. Seadragons are very sensitive to change and almost impossible to breed in captivity and, although some conservationists have successfully bred weedy seadragon, leafies have proved much more difficult. This is a cause for concern because, in a creature with such a limited distribution, it is important to have a captive breeding population to insure against sudden declines in numbers.

Seadragons lack the prehensile tail of other members of the seahorse family (notably, the pygmy seahorse, see pages 40–3), which means that they can't grip on to weeds and stems; this isn't true of the ruby seadragon, though, which might explain why it took so long to discover it – it is only very rarely washed onshore. A storm or rough sea makes seadragons susceptible to getting washed away or stranded on the coast. The group's sensitivity does have some plus points; seadragons are good at revealing subtle changes in environmental conditions that might be undetectable otherwise. This is called being an 'indicator species' by ecologists and environmentalists. Tragically, these fish are currently showing a drastic population decline, clearly indicating that something is not right off the south Australian coast.

In Sydney Harbour, there was a large population of common seadragons thriving right under the myriad piers and jetties, doing well despite the potential disturbance from boats and ships. However, a survey team used to turning up sixty individuals under just one pier reported seeing a mere eight in 2019. Scientists suspect climate change is the culprit. The gradually warming seas are not just uncomfortable but calamitous for a creature that is so sensitive.

We have to ask ourselves what a world would be like without seadragons. The answer is, surely, that it would be much less interesting.

The leafy seadragon goes almost over the top with all the extra fins and appendages. Hidden inside all that, there is a fish.

36 | SOCKEYE SALMON

{Oncorhynchus nerka}

A.K.A.

Red salmon, blueback salmon, *suk-kegh*

SIZE

60–84 cm (24–33 in)

HABITAT

From inland lakes and rivers to the Pacific Ocean

DISTINGUISHING FEATURES

Pointy snout

PERSONALITY

Extreme

LIKES

Travel and change

SPECIAL SKILLS

Swapping from saltwater to freshwater

CONSERVATION STATUS

Least Concern

EVERYTHING ABOUT THE salmon is extreme: not only do they embark on one of the most extraordinary life cycles in the world, but their entire bodies alter and change in the process (I wanted to include a picture of a non-breeding sockeye salmon to show you how different they start out – like the ugly duckling but in reverse!). That is the very reason I have included this famous fish in this section – very few animals perform such extreme transformations. However, it's not just their external physical transformation that makes the salmon so impressive; it's their internal ones, too.

Sockeye is one of five Pacific salmon species that migrate from freshwater, where it hatches, out to sea, only to return to its natal river a few years later to breed – a condition called anadromous, as we've seen with other species in this book. All of these salmon share the generic name of *Oncorhynchus*, which refers to their bizarre faces and means 'barb-snout' (I prefer 'pointy face'). They all go through some kind of transformation when they arrive back in the rivers to breed, although none is quite as extreme as the sockeye salmon. The others, all popular angling fish, have at least two names due to their familiarity with fishermen. They are pink or humpback salmon (*O. gorbuscha*), coho or silver salmon (*O. kisutch*), chum or dog salmon (*O. keta*) and chinook or king salmon (*O. tshawytschab*).

Even the sockeye salmon has a couple of alternative names: red salmon and blueback salmon, which, though they sound contradictory, refer to the breeding and non-breeding colours respectively. The name 'sockeye' is derived from Halkomelen name for the species (this is the language of the indigenous tribes along the Fraser River in British Columbia), which is *suk-kegh*, meaning 'red fish'.

From freshwater to seawater and back

As we have seen, all the Pacific salmon live in both saltwater and freshwater during their life cycles. All animals need to maintain constant levels of water inside their bodies and use a process known as osmoregulation. How this works is relatively simple: water naturally moves from areas of low concentrations to areas of high concentrations of ions and other essential chemicals. For fish living in any kind of water, osmoregulation plays a key role in staying alive every day – and whether you live in freshwater or saltwater determines how you go about it – so what happens if you live in both types?

In freshwater, the key is to prevent too much water from entering the

Salmon embark on one of the most extraordinary life cycles in the world.

cells (cells are more concentrated than the surrounding water, which means that water naturally wants in). You can't just close the door as cells do need some water, which contains all the minerals and trace elements they require. So fish like salmon have evolved an ingenious pump in their gills that extracts the chemicals they need and pumps out the rest. Kidneys also play a role here, and freshwater fish excrete very dilute urea to help keep the body balanced.

The big problem for salmon is when they go into a saltwater environment – then the whole world flips upside down. Now water naturally tries to leave the fish's body (the body cells are lower in concentration than the water around them, so the water tries to get out). Once again, that remarkable pump comes to the rescue. Salmon have evolved the ability to reverse the pump so that it actively pumps salts and other chemicals out, as do the kidneys, which now excrete very concentrated urea. This clever evolutionary trick means that anadromous salmon can live in two completely different worlds. The changeover is not instantaneous, however, and can take as long as twenty-four hours to kick in – this is why a substantial bottleneck can form at the mouth of many salmon rivers when they are leaving or returning – all of them are resetting their metabolic processes, like we used to do with our watches when entering a new time zone.

Reversing their osmoregulation is not the only thing salmon do that is seemingly miraculous. Sockeye salmon, like most other members of their genus, are also famous for returning to not only the same river but the very same pool – and even the same small area of riverbed where they were born – when ready to breed themselves.

They might well have not seen nor spent any time in that small location for at least four years – and sometimes longer. But return to it they do – merely to spawn and then die. This makes them 'semelparous' (the technical term for an animal that dies once it has spawned).

Anadromous salmon can live in two completely different worlds.

So much of a salmon's life cycle poses questions for which the answers are hard to discover. How they relocate their natal spawning grounds is believed to be done using magnetic forces in their cells and memory – although smell and sight may also play a role. In contrast, some salmon go against their programming and become pioneers, investigating new rivers they weren't hatched in.

Expendable parents

Dying after spawning may seem a little extreme – but recent discoveries have thrown some light on this behaviour, indicating that it is a harsh but sensible survival strategy. The cold highland streams the sockeye breed in are derived from natural springs and frequently bereft of essential elements. When the salmon die almost immediately after spawning – and they do so in their millions, often famously providing a glut of food for large birds and mammals – their rotting corpses seep phosphorus, nitrogen, calcium and magnesium into the water, enabling the next generation to absorb the essential nutrients they need – and it's not just the next generation of fish; the thousands of bears, wolves, sea eagles and even trees rely on this behaviour. A scientific experiment showed that the trees in the areas of the Pacific northern rainforests all thrive on marine-based phosphorus uptake that could only be derived from the salmon. Not only do these piscean miracle-workers transform their own bodies, giving up their lives for their future generations, they also feed the entire forest ecosystem that surrounds them – not only sustaining some of the greatest biodiversity on Earth but also one of the greatest carbon-dioxide sinks on our planet.

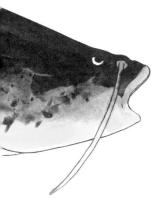

Chapter 6

LEGENDS
OF OLD

Everyone loves a dinosaur and I am no different; however, few people appreciate that there are plenty of fish species on this planet that were not only alive at the same time the dinosaurs roamed the land but were even around before them. This chapter features some of the most ancient and strangest fish on the planet. Prepare for astounding revelations from Earth, the early days.

37

ATLANTIC STURGEON

{*Acipenser oxyrhinchus*}

ANCIENT MONSTERS SUCH as the Atlantic sturgeon could perhaps be described as aristocratic giants that swam around the feet of dinosaurs. They certainly look antediluvian with their pinched, myopic-looking eyes, that drooping moustache and an armour-plated body like a medieval librarian-knight wearing a pince-nez. But sturgeon don't need such human trappings: those four barbels hanging down under the chin do all the sensing the fish needs as it cruises along the bottom of rivers, estuaries and coastal waters, hoovering up the food items it touches. 'Hoovering' as used here is not just a metaphor; these leviathans of the deep have extendable, though toothless, jaws that they use to suck in food. This feeding technique clearly works, as sturgeons and their ancestors have been using this method for many millions of years. Sturgeon fossils date back to the Triassic period (245–208 million years ago) – which is around the first time a mammal or near-mammal was seen on Earth, according to the fossil record.

*The sturgeon
is arguably
the biggest
freshwater fish
species on Earth.*

Burgeoning sturgeons

The Atlantic sturgeon lives along the coast of North America, from Florida to Canada – but it is not just restricted to that ocean. Sturgeon are another member of the anadromous gang (like salmon and eels) that migrate to and from freshwater to spawn. The species seasonally and historically inhabited thirty-eight rivers along the US Eastern Seaboard – although this has dropped to twenty-two in modern times; these include huge and famous estuaries such as the Chesapeake Bay and mighty rivers such as the Hudson – known as sturgeon rivers.

A big sturgeon can grow to 4.6 m (15 ft) and weigh as much as 363 kg (800 lb) and so is arguably the biggest freshwater fish species on Earth (although their sea-going habits probably preclude them from strict inclusion in this category). When these titans were first seen by pioneers exploring the New World, accustomed to fishing for brown trout (*Salmo trutta*) and wild Atlantic salmon (*Salmo salar*), they must have got quite a shock. At the time, sturgeon were so numerous that an early exaggerated account claimed someone might be able to walk across the James River, Virginia, on their backs.

This last claim is not as outlandish as you might think. These explorers would have witnessed the huge spawning gathering that happened during the late summer in the southern states and late spring in the more northerly regions. Spawning is what these guys do best – it is a fiesta. It is estimated that a single large female can lay 3.75 million eggs in a single year – but even smaller females can produce something in the region of 800,000 eggs.

Once spawning is completed, the males often linger to look after the fry for a short while as they grow, while the females head straight back out to sea. As a single sturgeon can live until it is sixty years old, sturgeon pack in a lot of eating, growing and egg-laying in a single lifetime. The young stay in the river systems for up to six years as they grow and mature, although the true length of time depends on how much food is available; having reached sexual maturity, they then head out in the ocean to grow some more.

The real threat

A defining feature of sturgeon is the presence of hard bony plates in rows along its spine and sides which are called scutes. These are modified scales that serve the purpose of protecting sturgeon from larger predatory fish and sea mammals as they grow up. Sturgeon lack true scales and, other than the scutes, are covered with a tough bluish-grey or green skin. The real threat to sturgeon comes – inevitably – from humans. We've created lots of problems for these fish, many which could, and still can, be avoided.

The eggs are very valuable, being better known as caviar.

While our tendency to poison rivers with pollution hasn't helped promote the cause of sturgeons, it is the construction of dams for hydroelectric power schemes without consideration for the migratory fish populations that has thwarted the fish's development. Preventing sturgeon (or any fish for that matter) from performing their annual ritual of heading up rivers to spawn is a full-blown calamity – no matter how many fish there are, if they are prevented from breeding, they quickly die out – whether by poisoning or old age – without producing offspring any species will rapidly become extirpated. The truth is we would be killing them anyway, without doing it inadvertently. Why? Well, spawning sturgeon lay eggs and those eggs are very valuable, being better known as caviar.

The new 'black gold'

While caviar is often thought of as a Russian delicacy, the caviar craze began in North America in the nineteenth century, when colonists began flocking to the Eastern Seaboard in a special kind of gold rush, a madness for a new kind of 'black gold': sturgeon eggs. The demand was devastating to sturgeon numbers. In 1887, an estimated 3.2 million kg (7 million pounds) of Atlantic sturgeon was caught from Canada down to Florida. That is the rough equivalent of about 500 adult bull elephants or fifty-two M1 Abrams tanks. Sturgeon meat became known as 'Albany beef', as it was popular, delicious, plentiful and served along with the more expensive roe as an accompaniment to 5-cent beer in local bars.

The exploitation of sturgeon was done without legislation or regulation, and attracted any chancer who wanted to make their fortune. No wonder, then, that by 1905 only 9,070 kg (20,000 lb) of sturgeon was being collected (which is roughly a mere ten tons or two African elephants and not even the gun turret or wheels of an M1 Abrams tank). Even so, the harvesting sputtered on until 1989 – the last annual total was a paltry 180 kg (400 lb). The Atlantic sturgeon was then considered endangered by the IUCN and has remained so ever since. Even worse, the whole twenty-seven-strong family is now considered the most critically endangered family on the planet.

The desire for caviar by many people continues unabated to this day, and once the US market had dried up, the market moved, which is why we now associate it with Russia. And as a 1-kg (2-lb-3-oz) tin of Beluga caviar can be sold for £20,000 ($34,000) that is a lot of money for some fish eggs – albeit from a rare and unusual albino beluga sturgeon. However, there is some good news: recent reports have suggested that there may now be one or two giants returning to the USA Eastern Seaboard rivers to breed. Let's hope that they are better looked after this time.

Tragically these are one of the most plundered animals on the planet.

38

MARBLED LUNGFISH

{Protopterus aethiopicus}

A.K.A.

Leopard lungfish

SIZE

Up to 2 m (6 ft 7 in)

HABITAT

Swamps, riverbeds and floodplains

DISTINGUISHING FEATURES

Long tapered tail

PERSONALITY

Adaptable

LIKES

Molluscs

SPECIAL SKILLS

Surviving out of the water for up to two years

CONSERVATION STATUS

Least Concerned

I HAVE TO SAY there is considerable satisfaction in painting this bizarre species of fish, which looks somewhat like a Moomin. It is also scientifically renowned for having the largest genome of any vertebrate on Earth (possessing 133 million base pairs, which are the fundamental units that build the DNA double helix). Marbled lungfish is also likely to survive any apocalypse we might care to throw at the world as it will be fully prepared for a barren world with no water; whatever happens, lungfish will be ready.

Also known as the leopard lungfish, this is one of four African species of lungfish and is rather a common species in Central Africa, found throughout the Congo and Nile river systems, as well as in all the Rift Valley lakes. It can grow to 2 m (6 ft 7 in) in length and has an entire body that seems to be composed of one giant muscle or beautifully patterned giant tongue. Its fins take the form of rather tiny flailing arms, giving it a hint of silliness. These specially adapted fins are very

The lungfish has an entire body that seems to be composed of one giant muscle.

practical however; if a lungfish finds itself out of the water, the fins rotate like a robotic arm to propel the fish back to the water – almost like legs. On occasion, a lungfish will even leave the water on purpose, deserting one muddy puddle for a better water body further away, being able to cross land for some distance, quite effectively.

Coming up for air

Originally named 'lungfish' because it was believed that these fish were able to breathe air just like us, it has been more recently discovered that lungfish can also breathe like 'normal' fish, too – absorbing oxygen from the water through gills. However, lungfish can also gulp air at the water surface, especially when the oxygen levels in the water drop so low that other kinds of fish suffocate. It is this trick that means lungfish are always the last to leave the party – and when they do, it is more of a disappearing act.

This is because lungfish have a survival plan like no other. When the water levels drop to a certain level and all the other fish in a river, pool or pond around them are gasping and flapping in their final throes, lungfish start digging, burrowing down into the soft mud. Once they have dug deep enough, they cocoon themselves by producing a thin, self-made mucus membrane – something like a slimy sleeping bag. Once ensconced inside, they shut down all of their metabolic and brain activity, and stay in suspended animation, waiting for better times.

This shutdown is technically termed 'aestivation' and is similar to the hibernation seen in some mammals. Lungfish can remain in this state for up to two years if they need to. The marbled lungfish is adapted to the African continent's two dramatic annual changes: the rainy and dry seasons (although, there is also a shorter rainy period near the end of the dry season, too, after which the dry season becomes hotter before the rainy season kicks in properly). Observers of dried-out waterholes, as they finally begin to fill with fresh rain after weeks, months or even years without water, will see dry hollows or muddy puddles turn into lakes – and then, suddenly, fish will appear, as if by magic. The aestivating lungfish were there all the time, waiting in the 'wings' underground for the seasons to change. Indigenous African hunters are, of course, well aware of them and have been known to occasionally dig them out for food – they are a great source of water and protein in a tough environment.

Better than beef

This seemingly miraculous trick has allowed the humble lungfish to enter the mythologies of many tribal societies. The Baganda people of Uganda believe the fish to be taboo – a magical animal that must be protected rather than eaten. However, others consider them as less magical and more edible, so they are fervently hunted and seen as the valuable source of protein they are. For the Luo people of Tanzania, they are called *kamangi yasinda nyama*, which translates as 'more delicious than beef'; lungfish are mostly only served at special occasions there. The Luo are not the only people that consider them tasty. Huge fisheries have been set up at East Africa's Lake Victoria targeting lungfish as a prize catch. And it's not just humans: that monolithic avian denizen of Central African wetlands, the shoebill – a kind of giant-headed stork and one of the largest and most impressive birds on Earth – is also partial to lungfish, as are, of course, the crocodiles and otters so

Lungfish are also used in traditional African medicine.

Able to survive years out of water, they are the original 'preppers'.

abundant in these rich African waterways.

Lungfish are also used in traditional African medicine to help cure everything from alcoholism and breast cancer to sexual dysfunction, although there is no scientific evidence to suggest that the fish contain any of the properties attributed to help with these medical issues. Lungfish, themselves, prefer to eat freshwater molluscs, with estimates suggesting that each fish can eat as many as 200 snails in one sitting. Unfortunately, snails are the intermediary host to the *Schistosoma* parasitic flatworm that impacts millions of people in Africa with a disease called bilharzia, or schistosomiasis – a disease for which 290 million people have to be preventatively treated every year, according to World Health Organization data, demonstrating how widespread it is in sub-Saharan Africa. So lungfish, despite being delicious to eat, play an important role in indirectly helping human health, by themselves eating a lot of the snails that contain the flatworms, thus preventing them from getting into humans.

Lungfish have now been on this planet for more than 400 million years – making them older than dinosaurs, older than flowering plants, older even than the continents. Our respect is more than due for this ancient and rugged survivor.

39

SEA LAMPREY

{Petromyzon marinus}

MEET THE MOST primitive fish on our planet. And when I say 'fish', I use that term loosely – this ancient lineage of jawless fish has no scales – only smooth skin; no gills – just slit-like openings on the side of its head; and no true fins like other fish – that is, no pectoral, pelvic or anal fins. As well as not having a jaw, lampreys are made of cartilage rather than bone, like sharks and rays. But lampreys are far from being simple relics; they are modern and successful fish that still hold their own many millions of years later.

Sucking blood

They have a few alternative names, the most exciting and memorable of which is certainly the vampire fish. They are obligate hematophages; in other words, they have to drink blood. There are very few fish which are truly parasitic bloodsuckers (see the candiru, pages 44–7, too – but lampreys are the long-standing originals).

There are thirty-eight species of lampreys known and described on the planet today but only eighteen of these feed on blood. The others generally live in freshwater as larvae, filter-feeding and transforming into their adult forms, then breeding and dying. The name 'lamprey' translates as 'stone sucker' or 'stone licker', from the Latin *lambere*, to lick, and *petra*, stone. This more than adequately describes their habit of attaching themselves to objects with their astonishing mouths to avoid being washed away. Lampreys have also been found to be one of the most efficient swimmers among fish, creating a lateral wave around their bodies so that the water itself literally pulls them along.

Of those eighteen species that get up to their bloodthirsty mischief, the sea lamprey is the biggest. Able to reach 1.27 m (4 ft 2 in) in length and weighing up to 2.27 kg (5 lb), they can be formidable parasites, attaching themselves to larger fish, sometimes in numbers. Like salmon, they head up rivers to breed. And like salmon, they even dig out 'redds' for their eggs – shallow depressions in the gravel of the stony riverbed, formed by the actions of the male's tail. The males then entice females with wafts of pheromones that float downstream, luring her to him. When she approaches, he leaves nothing to chance, producing attracting heat via a ridge of fat cells behind the anterior dorsal fins to further entice and excite her.

Once the eggs are laid, both parents die, leaving their rotting corpses to feed the next generation. Lamprey larvae are called 'ammoncetes' and take the form of tiny little tubes, drifting and floating around the river in almost planktonic fashion for a couple of years. Once grown to a suitable size and state, they migrate out to sea to transform into the grotesque (but beautiful) adult I've illustrated here.

Lampreys are made of cartilage rather than bone, like sharks and rays.

Dracula's goldfish

Key to a lamprey's survival is its bite – and their mouthparts are precisely designed to do just that. Their mouth consists of a single sucker and is one of the most grisly and gruesome parts of the body to be evolved by any animal. This alien mouth clamps on to the body of a fish using the suction pressure provided by the rubber rim of its mouthparts. Then the circular layered rows of teeth grip the victim's flesh and scales as the mouthparts rhythmically saw into the animal so tenaciously that the lamprey is almost impossible to pull off. Once in position, the lamprey, like a sharp, pointed rasp file, drills into the body of the fish, burrowing through the scales and musculature and into the blood system. An anticoagulant fluid called lamphredin, produced by the parasite's mouth, ensures that the blood runs freely. Lastly, the lamprey's swallowing actions create a pump to keep the blood flowing into its gut.

An average-sized adult lamprey is estimated to kill around 18 kg (40 lb) of fish during its adult life (it will exist for between 12–18 months). I say 'kill', because a fish that has been 'lampreyed' is unlikely to survive, due to infection or blood loss; if it does survive such attacks, it will be weakened by the gaping big hole in its side.

This feeding technique has been working for lampreys for millions of years, so they are unlikely to change any time soon. This apparent primitiveness doesn't mean the group has not been adaptable. In fact, some lampreys observed even at the beginning of the twentieth century demonstrated just how adaptable they could be.

Parasitic profusion

North America in the early 1900s was a land of opportunity for countless new immigrants. One of the huge, ambitious projects begun by the pioneers of the time was to construct a series of canals to connect some of the most amazing natural wonders of this new world: the five Great Lakes (Superior, Michigan, Ontario, Erie and Huron). Together, these lakes represent the greatest body of freshwater on Earth and hold more than a fifth of all the globe's freshwater. In 1919, the Wetland Canal was completed, connecting Lake Ontario with Lake Erie, while the last of the series of canals ultimately joined up all the lakes with the St Lawrence Seaway, bypassing Niagara Falls.

Not only did this present a whole host of new opportunities for human pioneers, but the most 'primitive' fish on the planet also found an opening suitable for exploitation. Sea lampreys began to invade the Great Lakes in their millions and, within a short decade, every lake had a population of bloodsucking, parasitic fish. The river ecosystems of Europe, Canada and the US were well adjusted to the presence of lampreys, with the local fish populations wary of them, having evolved alongside them for years, and a healthy parasite-prey balance was maintained. The Great Lakes, however, had no experience of lamprey and had huge water bodies stuffed with ecologically 'innocent' trout, perch and whitefish. The lamprey responded mercilessly and, within a century of having access, the lamprey had decimated the lakes' populations of trout – a business valued at $10 million a year, at one time. The lamprey was public enemy number one – possibly 'the most invasive species ever to hit homeland soil': a testament to their success.

Sea lampreys began to invade the Great Lakes in their millions.

40

WEST INDIAN OCEAN COELACANTH

{Latimeria chalumnae}

A.K.A.

Gombessa, African coelacanth

SIZE

Up to 2 m (6 ft 7 in)

HABITAT

Underwater caves

DISTINGUISHING FEATURES

Dark blue camouflage

PERSONALITY

Living fossil

LIKES

Night fishing

SPECIAL SKILLS

Staying out of sight

CONSERVATION STATUS

Critically Endangered

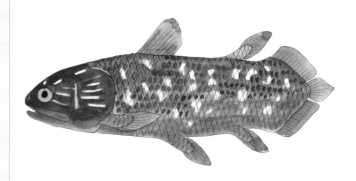

IF ANY OF the Earth's fish look primeval, it has to be the West Indian Ocean coelacanth. This is not just a superficial opinion – humans first encountered impressions of the coelacanth's close relatives trapped in stone, in fossilized remains, dating as far back as the early Carboniferous period (360 million years ago) – in fact, coelacanths are as old as lampreys. For a long time, experts believed that coelacanths had died 66 million years ago, during the last great extinction and the change between the Cretaceous and Eocene periods, until one day, out of the blue, one was found freshly dead among the catch of fisherman in East London, South Africa.

For a long time, experts believed that coelacanths had died 66 million years ago.

From lobes to legs

Before this momentous discovery (which we'll examine shortly), coelacanth were important fossil forms because of their 'lobed' fins. These fish appeared to be the evolutionary missing link between fish and tetrapods – that is, four-limbed animals such as amphibians, reptiles, birds and mammals. Everyone now knows that life began in the sea and then somehow dragged itself out on to land – coelacanths were the first fish to be discovered in the fossil record with the anatomy to pull something like that off. Coelacanths were fairly common as fossils and widely distributed, but it was believed that they had been extinct for millions of years, until one day that suddenly changed.

The date was 23 December 1938. Imagine, then, the surprise of a biology teacher called Marjorie Courtney-Latimer (who already knew all the theories about coelacanths and the beginning of vertebrate life on land) who, as she was walking through a local fish market looking for specimens for her small museum, came across what was obviously a very recently dead, metre-long coelacanth laying on a slab among the snappers and sardines caught by a fisherman named Captain Hendrick Goosen. Unsurprisingly, this fish stood out – it doesn't look like a carp with legs, but is a wide, solid, bulky, primitive-looking fish with large eyes, wide fins and (my favourite fish feature) an extra small tail fin set inside its larger, more typical tail. A coelacanth almost looks like it's carved out of wood, with chunky, diamond-shaped scales covering every inch.

Courtney-Latimer couldn't quite believe she was staring at a living fossil, a creature thought dead for 66 million years – except this one had quite clearly died that morning. She began to ask a flurry of questions while talking to the fisherman, asking how often he caught them and where, was this a typical size and, most importantly for the fisherman at least, how much did he want for it. Once she had drained her brain of questions and handed over enough money to secure it, she took her new prize home and called her boss, Mr J.L.B. Smith. Smith, a leading ichthyologist, understood without equivocation the importance of this find. He would go on to describe and officially name the creature, honouring its finder with a new generic name, *Latimeria*. It turned out that the fish had been caught off the Comoro Islands, near Madagascar, and we now know that its range extends from South Africa north to Kenya. It hides out in underwater caves between 180–243 m (590–797 ft) in depth during the day, emerging at night to feed on small fish and crustaceans.

Could they have used those limb-like fins for walking?

Primitive preservation

Right now, however, the two had a more immediate problem: the fish was beginning to smell due to the heat and climate of the South African summer; they clearly needed to get it to a fridge as quickly as possible – but who, in 1939 in South Africa, had a fridge that could fit a metre-long fish? They didn't want to cut it up, as they would lose too much valuable information and this specimen could quite possibly be the last one ever, as the fisherman at the market said coelacanths were only rarely caught. The local owner of a cold store was quickly drafted in, who had a fridge big enough for the whole fish. Finally, after the busiest day of her life, Ms Courtney-Latimer was able to rest, safe in the knowledge that she had been able to secure and preserve the most incredible biological specimen she – or anyone else, for that matter – was ever likely to find.

What she didn't know was that the next few days would be just as frantic and bizarre. Initially, many in the scientific establishment thought it a hoax or a joke, but with such a leading authority as Smith on board, it was soon properly heralded as a major discovery.

This was only the start. Now that people knew that coelacanths still existed, the search was on for more – and more there were, and not just one species. We now know that there are at least two extant species with the discovery of the Indonesian coelacanth (*L. menadoensis*) in 1997 (also found in a fish market!), which ranges through the deeper waters of around 150 m (490 ft) off the large islands of Sulawesi, Papua and West Papua.

Now that the species is more widely known and studied, it is even possible for people to dive with them. Familiarity has revealed that the fish is sexually dimorphic, males having a subtly beautiful royal blue skin with pale blue blotches, while females are larger and have a duller colouration. We also know that coelacanths are ovoviviparous – that is, they give birth to live young, after a year-long gestation period.

However, the biggest question surrounding the physiology of the coelacanth remains definitively unanswered: could they have used those limb-like fins for walking? These ancient fish are resolutely aquatic and are only ever hauled out of the water by fishermen. While we can't see this potential behaviour in the surviving coelacanth species, it's likely place in the ancestry of terrestrial tetrapods can be seen elsewhere: in its genes. DNA analysis has shown that the coelacanth is more closely related to tetrapod amphibians than it is to other bony fish (apart from lungfish). It seems that coelacanths really are the missing link after all!

Raised from the fossil bed, they are truly prehistoric-looking.

41

BLUNTNOSE SIXGILL SHARK

{Hexanchus griseus}

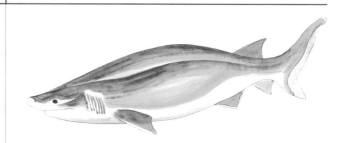

A.K.A.

Cow shark

SIZE

Up to 5.5 m (18 ft)

HABITAT

Deep ocean

DISTINGUISHING FEATURES

Six rows of serrated teeth

PERSONALITY

Scavenger

LIKES

Whale meat

SPECIAL SKILLS

Glowing eyes to see in the dark

CONSERVATION STATUS

Near Threatened

THIS IS ONE of the most mystifying sharks on our planet, with more fossil relatives than living ones. Although it is often called the cow shark, its life is not nearly as well known as the familiar domestic mammal. Even the question of how it reached 5.5 m (18 ft) in size is still mostly unanswered. The mysteries of the bluntnose sixgill sharks are largely kept secret owing to its preference for living at depths of up to 1,800 m (about 6,000 ft) and no one knows the true size of grown adults in the fathomless inky darkness; even so, this is one of the 'top ten' biggest sharks in the world.

Crushing pressure

The deep ocean is a tough place to live. It has crushing pressure, pitch darkness and extremely low oxygen levels; these facts beg the question of why any animal would live in the abyss in the first place. The answer is food. The abyssal waters and plain are a veritable candy store of edible treats – for one thing, it is estimated that there are almost 690,000 carcasses of dead whales at any one time at the bottom of the sea, providing the meat and carrion on which the ecology of this obscure but massive habitat is based. If an animal has evolved to handle all these major hindrances, it is well worth it for the variety of food available.

Bluntnose sixgill sharks are one of the main scavengers of the whale-fall from dead cetaceans. When a whale dies, it initially floats and is consumed by more familiar sharks on the sea surface. Once all the gases leave its now decomposing body, which can take several days, the corpse begins to sink in slow motion to the ocean floor. A dead whale has a particularly pungent allure, as you can imagine, and sea-floor scavengers find this utterly appealing and eminently detectible, homing in on it from miles away. The decaying whale is almost literally manna from heaven, remaining full of high-calorie food as it falls thousands of feet before its huge bones rest on the ocean's floor.

With such large food parcels arriving regularly, it's little wonder that 'bluntnoses' get to grow so big. Even so, their preferred habitat is the reason that we only really know what we can see from a remote camera or the window of a bathysphere or mini-submarine when they are feasting on whale carcases under hundreds of feet of water. Their large, blunt faces allow them to wedge their entire heads into the carcass to gain purchase on the tastiest morsels of muscle with their unusual jagged teeth (see 183). Then, with vigorous shakes of their monstrous heads, they can tear huge boulder-sized chunks of meat off the long-dead giant, before hurriedly gulping them down.

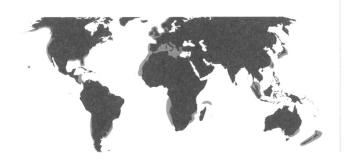

No one knows the true size of grown adults in the fathomless inky darkness.

Behemoth banquet

Cetacean-based banquets can attract huge numbers of these sharks and there are stories of submariners in small submersibles being barged out of the way by a bluntnose on its way to the sea-floor picnic blanket. The bluntnose's sharp pointy teeth also suggest that it will catch and eat living food of their own, and this is believed to include billfish, hagfish, octopi and squid. Even though we are only used to seeing bluntnoses languidly swim past a submarine, it seems they can move fast when they are hungry enough.

They can move fast when they are hungry enough.

While many other sharks have evolved blunt noses, they mostly have just five gills – although there also happens to be a broadnose sevengill shark which also lives in slightly less deep waters offshore. There are only three species of shark with six gills, include the equally mysterious, odd-looking but unrelated, frilled shark (*Chlamydoselachus anguineus*) and the bigeyed sixgill shark (*H. nakamurai*), which is in the same genus and found on the continental shelves of the Indian and western Pacific oceans. The generic name *Hexanchus* is derived prosaically from the ancient Greek *hex*, meaning 'six', and *anchus*, meaning 'bend' or 'bay' – perhaps a reference to the curvature of the gill slits.

Finding their way in the dark

Another big question about the lives of bluntnoses relates to how these giants navigate in the high-pressure darkness. They have quite prominent eyes which glow green in the dark but, with little to no light ever reaching the depths they live in, eyesight is not their main sense. It is generally assumed that they have an incredible sense of smell, like most other sharks. It has been proven that a shark can detect a single drop of blood in an Olympic swimming pool, so, if bluntnoses possess even part of that sensitivity, it would help them

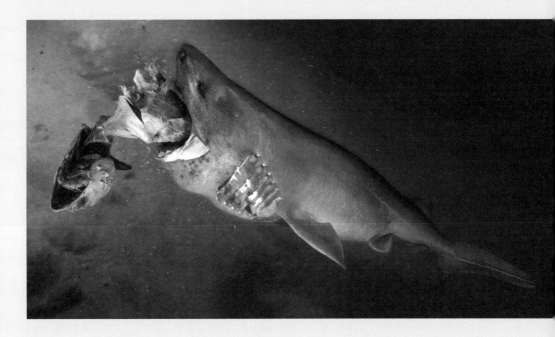

When they find food, they engulf it.

find food very effectively. The pungent emanations of a rotting whale should be easy for them to detect.

Although they live in incredibly deep waters, they are also one of the most widely distributed shark species on Earth, being found throughout the Atlantic Ocean, from Iceland to Namibia, and Brazil to West Africa. In the Indian and Pacific Oceans, they have been found from Madagascar to Japan, while one recently washed up on the shores of Vancouver, Canada, and another was filmed by an ROV over a wreck in the Philippines. They have even been seen around Greece and Malta, in relatively shallow seas, and a huge individual washed up on the shores of Turkey in 2019, weighing more than 400 kg (about 900 lb) and needing a crane to move it – so that is the Mediterranean, Aegean and the Black Sea covered. However, your only real chance of seeing live bluntnose will be from a submersible, if you manage to locate whale carcass.

I think it would be worth the effort, though: getting eye to glowing eye with one of our planet's most primitive, massive and mysterious sharks would be incredible!

42

SIAMESE FIGHTING FISH

{Betta splendens}

A.K.A.

Betta, bettah

SIZE

6–8 cm (2½–3 in)

HABITAT

River basins

DISTINGUISHING FEATURES

Flowing fins, bred with bright colours

PERSONALITY

Pugnacious

LIKES

Zooplankton and small crustaceans

SPECIAL SKILLS

Building nests

CONSERVATION STATUS

Vulnerable

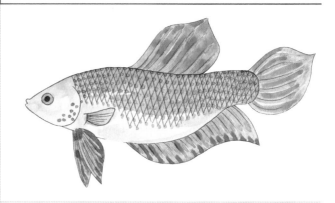

DRESSED LIKE A Spanish flamenco dancer, this attractive and ostentatious species is surely one of the most recognizable aquarium fish on Earth. It is also, as its name suggests, one of the most aggressive fish in existence – a behavioural trait that once made them an international obsession.

Its scientific name translates as 'beautiful warrior,' the Bettah being a warrior tribe from South-east Asia and *splendens* being, well, 'splendid' or 'beautiful'. Hopefully, their fighting days are behind them, and they are now bred and paraded in show fish tanks all over the world as one of the most exquisite members of the family Osphronemidae, which also contains about 133 other brightly coloured *gourami* species. However, our obsession with them started a long time ago, and it was all about their fighting abilities.

Piscean pugilists

The early eighteenth century, around the time of the Thonburi era, under the rule of King Rama III, is where we find the first historical indication of the human fixation with this fish. There are records of local legislation stating that people were not to gamble and that taxes were to be levied on fish fights, strongly suggesting that Siamese fighting fish must have been incredibly popular well before that. The king even collected his own champion fish at that time.

The story goes that this obsession began as a children's game. Kids would catch these pretty fish, put them in an urn or pitcher and watch and cheer as they battled it out, with a village winner being declared at the end of the day. This small fish must have been common enough for the kids to notice its natural aggression and that probably happened because Siamese fighting fish are often found in paddy fields. Rice is a staple in South-east Asia, but to grow it you need lots of water. Paddy fields are essentially agricultural marshlands, providing habitat for numerous wetland species, including amphibians, birds and fish.

This managed biodiversity is often encouraged, as not only do you have rice growing, you also have fish to catch. The fish are consumers of mosquito and other insect larvae, which in turn keeps plagues of biting insects at bay. This is the most likely place that children would have encountered Siamese fighting fish in their daily lives and witnessed their enthralling territorial behaviour. The children would have been expected to help their parents farm the paddies as they grew up, so spending time in the fields would have been quite normal.

It is, as its name suggests, one of the most aggressive fish in existence.

Even so, finding engaging distractions is still something inherent in all of us, and setting up fish fights would have been, above all, fun.

A wild Siamese fighting fish is relatively dull in colour. It is still beautiful, but probably pales in comparison to the showcased examples we see nowadays. It has to have been the fighting behaviour that drew the fish to our attention. Once the tradition of children setting matches was established, it can't have taken long for adult men in the village to start putting small wagers on the outcome of the matches. Eventually, gambling on fighting fish became a Thai national pastime.

It wasn't until 1840, when King Rama III had his own stable of fighting fish, that things went fully global. The king shared some fish with a collector, which then reached a Danish doctor named Theodore Edward Cantor, who was working in Bengal, India. He described and named the species *Macropodus pugnax* in 1850, from the Latin for 'fighter with big feet' (the fins being limbs of a sort). However, Cantor did not realize that this name had already been given to East Asian paradisefish, also used for fighting matches in China where they go

under the general name of 'Chinese bettas', owing to their superficial similarities with Siamese fighting fish. The latter had to be given a revised name, and, in 1909, Charles Tate Regan renamed the species *Betta splendens* after the legendary warriors.

So what is all the fighting about? The male Siamese fighting fish do battle over territories. Two males start the fight by facing off against each other – famously, they are so aggressive that they will even do this reflexively to their own reflections. The show begins with each flaring its gill covers, or opercula, before darting in to take chunks out of each other (the Thai name for the species

Fighting fish, or bettas, now come in an array of dazzling colours.

is *pla-kat*, translating as 'biting fish'), until one of them gives in and moves away, sometimes heavily wounded or dying. This is easier in the wild than in a fish tank, where there is much less room to move. Females seem to be almost as obdurate as the males, and quite happily fight with each other, too. However, in the wild, females left to their own devices form a hierarchy of dominance and arrive at a hard-won peace, rather than fight to the death.

Natural bubble tea

Despite this renowned pugilism, there is a gentle, almost artistic side to the Siamese fighting fish. It creates the most intricate nests, with males using air to produce mats of bubbles just on the surface of the water. There, he woos females in a courtship dance before they wrap themselves up in what is termed a nuptial embrace. Females indicate their willingness to breed by changing colour, producing vertical stripes down their sides. When the female releases her eggs, the male fertilizes them as they float into the bubble nest above. If any drop down, the male grabs them with his mouth and pushes them back into the bubbles to keep them safe. Females have been seen to support this endeavour but, unfortunately, often eat the eggs instead; this is probably why the male usually chases the females off once the eggs have all been laid. There can be as many as forty eggs tucked away in the delicate bubble nests, and after just thirty-six hours, the eggs hatch out into minuscule fry, still with their yolk sacs attached to feed themselves. The fry can stay in the bubble nest for a couple more days while the male prowls beneath, guarding them against predators and troublemakers.

Siamese fighting fish create the most intricate nests.

So ingrained into Thai society and history is the sport of fish fighting, it's no wonder the species has recently been declared the national animal of Thailand. If you consider that Thailand also has Indian elephants and tigers living wild in its countryside, I think you can see that this is a very high and well-deserved accolade.

43

BARRAMUNDI

{Lates calcarifer}

VERY FEW FISH have legends written about them,
are so taxonomically and sexually confusing and
yet are as globally recognizable as this one. The species
is particularly renowned in Australia – and that prefix
of 'barra' seems as antipodean as can be – but this fish
is a well-travelled species.

The barramundi is also known as the Asian sea bass
and is found throughout the Indo-West Pacific region.
More specifically, it can be found around India, where
it is known as *bhekti* in Bengali, and Sri Lanka, where
it is called *modha* in Singhalese and *keduwa* in Tamil. It
is found right down through South Asia (*maan cho* in
Cantonese, *cabah* in Javanese) and even as far north as
Japan (*akame*) and the Philippines (*solong-solong*) – and
right across Northern Australia.

Their dorsal spines can give an unwary fisherman a proper stab.

Fish on a larger scale

The name *barramundi* is an Aboriginal word that translates as 'large-scaled river fish'. Technically, the name barramundi originally referred to the unrelated southern and northern saratogas (*Scleropages leichardti* or S. *jardinii*, respectively) – but these two species are really Australian arowanas (see pages 142–5); it was also used to refer to Australian lungfish (see pages 168–71). However, that changed in the 1980s when the name was officially appropriated by *Lates calcarifer*, for the sole reason that it was a great advertising tool to sell the pure-caught Australian fish within the domestic market.

The 'barra' is pretty versatile and, thus, a real contradiction in terms. It prefers calm, clear water but can be found in turbid, fast-flowing freshwater streams. It is also quite at home in saltwater. It can be found along the coast, in lagoons or rivers, in mangroves or far out at sea. As long as the climate is warm – between 26–30°C (79–86°F) is best – then it is happy to live just about anywhere.

Their robustness and flexibility make the species very important for people living and working on the sea and coast. Some rely on them almost exclusively for protein in their diet – and as they are quick-growing (being sexually mature within three to four years) and can reach weights in excess of 60 kg (130 lb), they can make a good meal for many people at once. The barramundi is also now one of the most common sea fish to find on an Australian menu. It is not defenceless, being armed with up to nine dorsal spines along its back, with three at the rear among the anal fins and others on the operculum and among the other fins. It isn't poisonous like many other spiny fish, but these defences certainly stop other fish from attempting to eat them and can give an unwary fisherman a proper stab if they get the chance.

A lover's genesis

Barramundi is one of the few fish that has its own 'origin' myth. Although there are slight variations, the general story, as told by the aboriginal people of the Northern Territories in Australia, is romantic and centres around two young lovers. In the time before fish were created, there were two young lovers that ran away, spurred on because the girl, Yalima, was supposed to marry one of the elders of the tribe and didn't want to; she was already in love with a young man named Boodi from the same tribe. The whole tribe gave chase after the two eloping lovers because, in such society, to go against

Barramundis can change sex; they can be both male and female.

the elders was not only disrespectful but also punishable by death. The couple made it as far as the coast but became trapped between the sea and the high cliffs at their backs. They valiantly tried to fend off the tribe with their spears but were hopelessly outnumbered, and decided there was only one way to escape: they jumped off a cliff into the sea below, followed by several well-aimed spears from the disgruntled mob. They were never seen again.

It was said, however, that the Great Spirit intervened and, as the couple hit the water, fused them together to create one large fish that could hide in the mangroves – that is, the barramundi (though which particular species of this catch-all name is referred to is unknown). The spines on its back and in its fins represented the spears that had pierced the star-crossed couple as they made their leap. This tale marks how important the barramundi was to the people of the Northern Territories (and, indeed, still is). What is equally fascinating – though not too surprising, as the people of the land are very observant and perfectly in tune with nature – is how this tale also encompasses one of the most unusual traits of these fish: barramundis can change sex; they can be both male and female.

The best of both worlds

All barramundi hatch out as males. As they grow, on reaching three to four years old, they can turn into females. At breeding time – which is signified like a romantic novel at around the start of the monsoon on a new full moon – the males make their way down their river homes towards the estuaries and coasts, where the females are waiting for them. They spawn together en masse by releasing millions of eggs and sperm into the sea simultaneously. They are called 'broadcast spawners', which means they are using sheer luck and numbers to guarantee that at least some of the eggs will get fertilized, while the others distract predators. Once this annual dance is over and the task of fertilization complete, the male barramundi head back upriver to their feeding territories.

However, this is not true of all of them. Some males – usually the bigger, more mature ones – stay behind, where they transform from males into females, the saltwater being an important trigger in this unusual metamorphosis. Essentially, the bigger the barra, the more likely it is to become a female. This cycle continues once the new eggs have hatched and the surviving young barramundis start heading up the rivers to live their early years as males.

The colour of their scales can vary depending on their environment.

44 | WELS CATFISH

{Silurus glanis}

THIS FRESHWATER GIANT is almost summoned from our worst nightmares. It looks like a mythical Chinese dragon with its huge wide mouth and whiskers dangling like a grisly moustache (it is those whiskers that give the catfish family its English name, as you may have guessed). It has tiny, set-back eyes that glow in the dark when light is shone into them – an effect that derives from possessing a tapetum lucidum. This is the same reflective internal surface at the back of the eye that real cats have, which makes light bounce back immediately so that the eye receives twice the amount of light available, enabling the animal to see in sometimes extremely dark and murky conditions.

Ogre in the mud

This fish has spawned many legends and fairy tales but, like most aquatic animals, we have only ever seen glimpses of them, such as a long, amorphous, sinuous body in the mud, like a giant aquatic slug quickly disappearing below the surface – or by seeing a hapless bird or other small animal get sucked under by something dark and terrifying below. There is something about this fish that has historically stirred the imaginations of the people of the central European countries the fish calls home.

Wels catfish is the most unlikely of fish to have developed a fan club, but its popularity has led to it being introduced right across the planet. From the UK, where the species was introduced to Woburn Abbey in 1880, all the way to China, with Spain and France along the way.

This prevalence is not because it is a tasty addition to our diets (although small ones are relatively edible). A wels catfish is a slow-growing waste-disposal unit, that given time and the right conditions can grow into an absolute behemoth. The largest individuals have been estimated at 5 m (16 ft), and weighing in at around 300 kg (660 lb) – placing it among the biggest freshwater fish on the planet; it is certainly the largest in Europe. As you might expect from a fish that is sometimes caught by anglers, there are claims of much larger individuals, though few are authenticated; perhaps the most reliable claim of a giant is one of 144 kg (317 lb) and 2.78 m (9ft 1 in), fished out of the Adriatic coastal waters of the Po Delta in Italy.

Given time and the right conditions, it can grow into an absolute behemoth.

Roaming big cat

It is a rather territorial species, taking up life-long residence in its favoured large, warm lakes and deep, slow-moving rivers. Once one is located, it can be reliably found in the same place for as long as it lives – and it has a lifespan of fifty years or more. A wels catfish will roam some distances when foraging for food, but its catholic diet usually means it can find its preferred annelid worms, molluscs, crustaceans and insects close to home. However, a recent natural history documentary showed an introduced population of wels catfish in France that have developed their own hunting style: they have taken to snatching drinking pigeons, shooting up the beach or mud bank to snatch them before they can fly away. A terrifying sight if you are a bird, and it proves that these fish are not sluggish monsters but active and creative predators.

The barbels are also packed with taste buds.

It is a perfectly designed and incredibly sensitive beast when it comes to awareness of the world around them. Its body in some ways resembles – and in common with many other catfish species – a huge tongue, with over 250,000 taste buds found all over its body, so very little escape a wels catfish when it comes to taste and smell. Humans only possess a paltry 2,000 taste buds and they are all in our mouths.

Also in common with other catfish are the wels' barbels, with two obvious long cat-like strands on the top lip of the upper jaw and four shorter tufts on the lower jaw, just underneath. These 'facial tentacles' are incredibly versatile, with the longer ones on the top of the mouth waved around to feel their way through the dark muddy waters of a temperate river bottom or lakebed. Like the rest of its body, the barbels are also packed with taste buds to help pinpoint the direction from which smells and tastes are coming; it's hard to imagine this blind but sensorily stimulating worldview, but it is incredibly successful for catfish. Catfish also have great night vision as we've established – but it's the wels' sense of hearing that surprised scientists the most when it was examined.

Sensory success

The wels catfish has incredibly accurate and sensitive hearing, having evolved an ingenious feature called the Weberian organ, which connects its swim bladder to its ears. The swim bladder acts as an amplifier so that even the slightest noise can be heard by a wels catfish – and, remember, water is already a very good sound transmitter. We don't usually think of fish as using sound underwater, but it must provide a useful extra advantage when locating prey in the dark. Certainly, some fish and most cetaceans use sonar in the oceans for locating objects, prey and for communication – it seems logical, then, that a large, sedentary predator might also develop this ability.

This remarkably varied sensory ability and simple but robustly effective body pattern has made catfish – and particularly the wels catfish – one of the most successful animal families on Earth. The wels is one of the biggest but only one of a few that lives in Europe. In the Americas, the family has really branched out, with most of the estimated 3,000 species evolutionarily radiating into thirty-six families. The catfish family is among the elite evolutionary success stories of modern times.

They may not look like it, but they are fearsome predators.

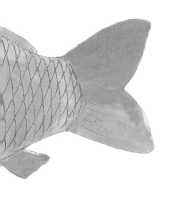

———— *Chapter 7* ————

WORLD
TRAVELLERS

As you are aware, fish are limited to aquatic habitats (although, as seawater covers 71 per cent of the globe, this is not that much of a limitation). However, even the most seemingly isolated species can go on amazing journeys and adventures around the world, for many different reasons. Some occasionally enlist the help of humans, while others undertake lengthy global migrations of their own volition. In this section, we will meet some of the most familiar fish that also have been on some of the most remarkable journeys, taking them far from home and bringing them to very unexpected places. All of them have fascinating stories to tell.

45

BROWN TROUT

{Salmo trutta}

A.K.A.

Sea trout, *sewin* (Welsh)

SIZE

Up to 1.4 m (4 ft 7 in)

HABITAT

Migrates from freshwater to the ocean

DISTINGUISHING FEATURES

Changing colours

PERSONALITY

Explorer

LIKES

Frustrating anglers

SPECIAL SKILLS

Metamorphosis

CONSERVATION STATUS

Least Concern

THIS SPECIES IS one of the most widespread freshwater fish on Earth and is found from Australia to the Falkland Islands, and from Canada to Tasmania. Bundled up inside it is one of the greatest concentrations of diverse genetic material that exists in any vertebrate on the planet. Brown trout are designed for a life of possibilities – even though they did get a helping hand.

Its natural distribution was already fairly large, as it is found wild and native in freshwater rivers from Iceland to the Atlas Mountains of North Africa. However, deep in its heart (and its DNA) it is a traveller and wanderer. How does a small freshwater fish get around so much? The answer to that is another fish species entirely, the sea trout. The brown trout and sea trout are the same species (and there may well be a few more guises hidden within the *Salmo trutta* identity – but more of that later).

Shapeshifting pioneers

Like salmon, a group of brown trout, or just an individual, will one day set out on a migratory mission and become sea trout in the process. What triggers this is something of a mystery. Some experts claim that it is mostly the females that transform (to grow faster on a diet of marine wonders and develop more eggs), but this is not proven. They do return after a period of time to breed once more in their home rivers. It's believed they might not travel as far as the salmon folk, once they get to the sea. Some even just stay in the estuary and are referred to as 'slob trout' – a fish after my own heart. And others may not return to their home rivers either. Scientists have found that many sea trout may be pioneers and travel in search of new opportunities in new river systems.

This species is one of the most widespread freshwater fish on Earth.

In basic terms, once on its journey inland, if a sea trout finds a new lake, river or stream full of food and without much competition, it becomes a brown trout again and stays put. This is how they can colonize new territories so easily – if things don't work out, they can just change back into sea trout and set off for greener pastures. This amazing genetic predisposition is essentially a 'get out of jail free' card in any situation and so it is no surprise that the species is so widespread.

Species within a species

Recent studies have turned up even more startling variability within a single population of brown trout living in just one lake. Ichthyologists went looking for another trout species, Arctic char, in a big Scottish loch, using large nets set at different depths to increase their chances of catching some. What they turned up was not what they were expecting at all. They didn't find any char – but, rather, four different 'types' of brown trout that all lived in their own separate small 'villages' in one loch without intermingling.

The first type were surface feeders living along the lakeshore; the second, surface feeders that lived out in the open water; the third (and these were the real surprises) were deep-water feeders; and the fourth was the monster of them all – the ferox trout (which is the form I have drawn for you). These atypical beasts act like pike, hunting and eating their own kind. However, all lived in ecological balance with each other in the same Scottish loch, all breeding in their own little pockets and rarely coming across one another. This is surely one of the most remarkable displays of local evolution to be seen – and one in a lake that Charles Darwin fished on when he was a boy, not knowing that one of the best examples of his theory of natural selection was happening right under his boat. To the possible relief of his ghost, these four trout forms were only discovered in 2009 using modern techniques unavailable to him at the time.

A brown trout can live for about twenty years.

This intricate evolutionary trickery did not get them everywhere around the globe, though. While they are native to the northern hemisphere, establishing a population in the Falkland Islands would be a long shot, even for a sea trout.

A trout's companion

The explanation for the current global range of brown trout is that we gave them a huge helping hand. As the West invaded and colonized and made most of the world part of someone or other's empire, we brought many home comforts along with us, even to some of the most remote outposts. In many cases, this involved the brown trout, introduced to native rivers and lakes to provide a familiar quarry for angling – and, indeed, a familiar flavour for dinner. Introductions of this species have been made to Australia, New Zealand, South Africa, Malawi, Kenya, the Falkland Islands, Chile, Argentina, Canada and the United States, making it one of the most widespread vertebrates in the world; it's the house sparrow or common starling of the fish world, in many respects.

We don't yet know what impact this might have had on native species, as most of the introductions happened long before we understood the full implications in terms of the environmental catastrophes that can be caused by invasive alien species – however, it's unlikely that the effects were good. The result is almost always a tragic epitaph for local flora and fauna – and with the brown trout's set of genes, it will take a miracle to eradicate it, once it is established.

A brown trout can live for about twenty years, breeding every year, and growing to upwards of 18.6 kg (about 41 lb) – the current world record for a rod-caught fish. Catching trout is a favourite human occupation – we didn't introduce them around the world for food as there was plenty in the rivers and lakes already; we introduced them because we love to try to catch them. There is a quote from an ancient Roman claiming the Macedonians liked to catch 'speckled fish' (a.k.a. trout) from around AD 200. Nowadays, trout fishing is a passion (and, indeed, a homewrecker!) for millions of people across the world – as well as an industry worth millions of pounds, with enough gadgets and equipment to keep even the most obsessive of anglers trying out gear forever.

The pursuit of trout is a calling and, therefore, it is little wonder that they have been transported to the far corners of the world just so we can be near them.

Here is a sight that would excite most anglers.

46

ATLANTIC BLUEFIN TUNA

{Thunnus thynnus}

A.K.A.

Northern bluefin tuna, tunny

SIZE

Up to 3m (10 ft)

HABITAT

Mid-waters of the Atlantic Ocean

DISTINGUISHING FEATURES

Warm-blooded

PERSONALITY

Gregarious

LIKES

Travel

SPECIAL SKILLS

Can reach a speed of up t0 64 kph (40 mph)

CONSERVATION STATUS

Endangered

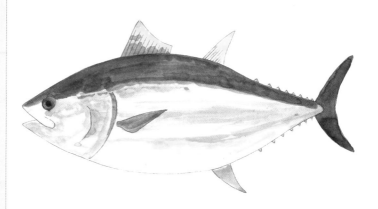

THE ATLANTIC BLUEFIN tuna is probably the most pursued fish in its nominal ocean – not the most fished for, trawled or hunted, but, literally, the most chased after. It is a predatory giant and the largest member of the tuna family. Atlantic bluefin tuna can reach 3 m (almost 10 ft) in length and weigh in excess of 450 kg (nearly 1,000 lb). It is a very sociable species, shoaling in its hundreds. The schools rampage around the top and mid-storeys of the ocean water column at incredible speeds, chasing mackerel and herring shoals, eating squid and even crabs, while trying to keep out of the way of orcas, fast sharks and, most of all, human fishermen.

Tuna triplets

There are now three species of bluefin tuna recognized globally, where once there was believed to be just one: the Atlantic, the Pacific (*T. orientalis*) and the southern (*T. maccoyii*) – the southern is only found in the oceans around the Capes and Antarctica. Modern genetic sampling reveals just how different the three forms are, with separate, distinct populations that do not interbreed. Even the Atlantic species is divided into two distinct subpopulations in the east and west of its Atlantic range. Eastern Atlantic bluefin tuna are found as far north as Norway and as far south as the Moroccan coast and, although they do feed and mix with the western population in the mid-Atlantic, eastern tuna choose the Mediterranean Sea to breed.

The western Atlantic bluefin tuna can be found cruising at high speed all along the North American coastline, from Canada down to the Caribbean; once there was a Brazilian population, although tragically, this has been completely fished out and hasn't been seen for almost forty years. The western tuna breed in the Gulf of Mexico, more than 6,000 miles from the eastern form.

Like a high-speed racing car, the Atlantic bluefin comes with some very specialized accessories. It has 8–10 sharp, bright yellow barbs running down its back and a retractable dorsal fin that can be raised or lowered according to how fast it wants to travel (and fast it is, being able to reach speeds of up to 64 kph / 40 mph). How it achieves such incredible speeds is down to several key factors: firstly, the species is shaped like a rocket, streamlined and top heavy to reduce the drag of the heavy

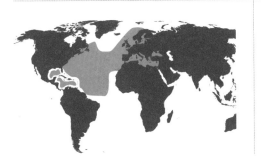

Like a high-speed racing car, the Atlantic bluefin is very streamlined.

seawater as it propels itself forwards with that flat, knife-like tail; secondly, it is warm-blooded or endothermic, making it different from most other fish, which are ectothermic or cold-blooded – having warmer blood means it can move quickly, generating its own bursts of energy. As long as it is eating well and topping up its engine, it can move faster and quicker than any other animal around them – particularly when under threat or hunting. Bluefin tuna can accelerate into shoals of smaller fish and pick off individuals, like cops in a high-speed car chase.

Their sociability is one of their main weaknesses.

Bigeyes and skipjacks

The tuna genus (*Thunnus*) has five more members, in addition to the three bluefin tuna. Their English names are catchy and to the point. Bluefins themselves do, indeed, have blue fins. The yellowfin tuna has yellow fins, the bigeye tuna has a big eye, blackfin tuna has a black upper half to its body and the longtail tuna has proportionately smaller frontal fins, making its tail at least look longer. Lastly, there is the albacore, with a Portuguese name that literally translates as 'a tuna', while being the smallest members of the family.

They all have one thing in common in a human context: they make up one of our favourite foods. According to pew.org, the commercial value of the tuna family is estimated to be as much as US $41.6 billion (£30 billion) to consumers, a significant amount of money in anyone's book. An individual large tuna is, pound for pound, more valuable than gold. When you realize that a big bluefin can weigh over 450 kg (1000 lb), that is the equivalent of a lot of gold. In January 2019, a single fish weighing 278 kg (612 lb) was purchased by a Japanese tycoon for US $3.1 million (about £2.5 million), which works out at about £15,482.60 per kg (£34,084 per lb); the rate at the time of writing for 28.35 g (1 oz) of gold at the time of writing was is

£1,218 ($1,687) per oz, making tuna about thirty times more valuable than gold by weight. No wonder people are obsessed with tuna!

Tuna ranching

This obsession with Atlantic bluefin tuna has led some entrepreneurs to begin 'ranching' them. How do you ranch a fish, you may ask? The tuna ranchers catch some young bluefins and put them into a giant net that hangs off the back of a big boat. They then drive these boats with their trailing nets around the Mediterranean, all the while feeding the shoal inside and moving so that the fish get plenty of exercise to keep their rich red blood flowing. The nets are big enough to house a jumbo jet, so it's quite a task to keep these nets in motion, but they do, for the entire period of one to two years that it takes before the fish are ready to be harvested. This process entails dragging the fish onboard one after the other, then killing and freezing them, before sending them to Japan (so that billionaire tycoons can pay ridiculous sums of money for them, of course).

Such commercial exploitation at least takes the pressure off the wild stocks, but it can be a tricky and expensive business. What if your net breaks and all the fish escape? Trained divers need to be employed to constantly check the nets underwater. Another issue is that ranching is fraught with exploitation: many reports indicate that more fish get to the market than have been genuinely legally farmed in these ranches. The only place these excess fish can come from is the wild.

However, it's not all bad news. The ICAAT (the International Commission for the Conservation of Atlantic Tuna) has laid out clear guidelines to protect the Atlantic bluefin and blackfin tuna populations, helping to reduce quotas and allowing the fish to breed, feed and swim fast without risk of being turned into sashimi. Within the first five years of this protection – bearing in mind tuna take ten years to reach maturity – the populations have fortunately increased significantly. As long as proper regulation of the fishing stocks and industry are adhered to, then these populations will stand a chance.

47

GOLDFISH

{*Carassius auratus*}

IT'S IMPOSSIBLE TO know how many pet goldfish there are in the world but these fish are undoubtedly the most recognizable for most people in the northern hemisphere, at least. From fairgrounds to ornamental ponds, these orange-coloured pocket jewels are one of the most popular aquarium fish – but their story began in China more than 1,000 years ago.

Originally, of course, it was all about food. These members of the carp family were kept in ponds by people in China (where they are native) for thousands of years as food. They can accidentally throw up a weird colour morph every so often – a red, gold or orange individual, born from the natural drabber brownish colouration of its parents.

These novel colours almost certainly encouraged the ancient Chinese to keep them as pets once commercial food fisheries for carp had become established – this was first known during the Jin dynasty (AD 265–460). This happened to such an extent that, when important people came to visit a house or town during the later Tang dynasty (AD 618–907), the most 'gold' of the fish would be popped into a small container and placed in the most visible place in a household, so that the visitors could admire it. Essentially, what we know as the pet goldfish was already in existence by then.

No one else could keep the yellow goldfish, as yellow was thought to be the emperor's colour.

However, during the Song dynasty (AD 960–1279), in 1172, Empress Wu decided that no one else could keep the yellow goldfish, as yellow was thought to be the emperor's colour. Once the fish became the province of royalty, it was inevitable that it would be declared fashionable – and thus began the global phase of the history of the goldfish. The species arrived in Portugal in 1611 (the Portuguese being the Europeans most connected to the mysterious Orient, at the time) and, from there, it travelled throughout Europe, arriving in the United States at around 1850, where it quickly became popular, like everywhere else.

Fairground attraction

The goldfish remains popular today and, as with most other domestic animals and pets, we have begun to properly mess with its genetic nature. The modern goldfish is one of the original genetically modified creatures. Goldfish are selectively bred for their shapes, characters and even colours. Instead of an instantly recognizable single fish breed, we now have fan-tailed, bubble-eyed and lion-headed versions of a goldfish, commonly available through dealers and pet suppliers. There are black, orange, bright red, speckled, dotted and even pearl-scaled goldfish. Some of them are as far removed from the original blueprint as a chihuahua is from a wolf (and just like a chihuahua, most of these goldfish variants wouldn't last more than a night in the wild). These manmade oddities are collected, sought after, and bought and sold sometimes for small fortunes. The more novel they are, it seems, the more we want them in our fairground trophy bags and home aquariums.

The goldfish's global domination has also meant that they sometimes turn up in unexpected places – and have been introduced into ponds and lakes all around the world, sometimes growing into real monsters; clearly, some of the breeds can survive in the wild! The biggest one ever caught is as controversial a subject as ever with anglers, but there are several on record that have weighed more than 9 kg (about 20 lb). This is less surprising than you might think if you bear in mind that the goldfish is a species of carp – many of which are frequently caught as game fish. Of course, the commoner, more natural (outside China) carp species are less flamboyant in colour. Just don't confuse them for koi, as those are a Japanese speciality derived from another species, the Amur carp.

The goldfish has rather a good memory. It can be trained to recognize faces.

Its colouration is not the only facet of the goldfish that has allowed it to conquer the world. It is remarkably adaptable, confident and catholic in its feeding habits; it will eat almost anything. One of the biggest threats to any pet goldfish is overfeeding as, like many other fish species, it does not know when it is full. As long as there is food present, it will keep eating – often to the point of organ failure, if left unchecked! In the wild, too much food is rarely an issue, so ensuring that it makes the most of what food there is, because it doesn't know where its next meal might come from, makes survival sense – though this impulse is also what makes it, in captivity, continue eating long past the point of satiation.

Forget what you know

However, the idea that the goldfish has a five-second memory is nonsense. While it is true that living in an actual goldfish bowl might well have driven the fish mad by making them constantly swim in circles, when it comes to memory, the opposite is true. The goldfish has rather a good memory. They can be trained to recognize faces and are generally much smarter than anyone considered, being able to remember tricks. The small, round glass containers traditionally holding goldfish were just meant to be temporary display tanks rather than permanent homes for this active species.

Hybrids with all manner of shapes, colours and sizes are now available.

We can now see that not only have these colourful characters conquered the world from the simplest of beginnings in rural Chinese ponds thousands of years ago, they have done it in style.

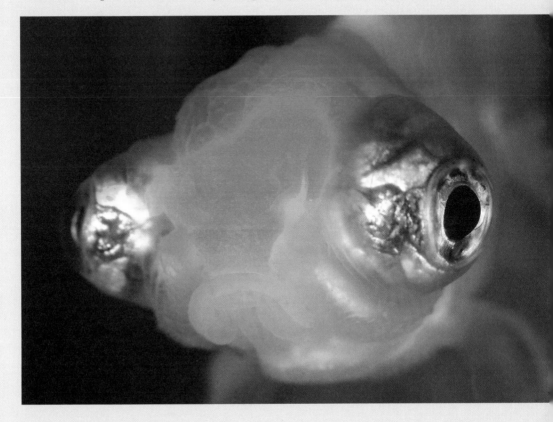

48

SARDINE

{Sardina pilchardus}

A.K.A.

European pilchard

SIZE

Around 20 cm (8 in)

HABITAT

Worldwide

DISTINGUISHING FEATURES

Long and thin

PERSONALITY

Sociable like you wouldn't believe

LIKES

Zooplankton and phytoplankton

SPECIAL SKILLS

Forming huge shoals

CONSERVATION STATUS

Least Concern

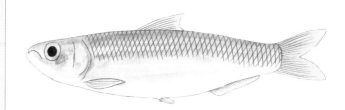

THE SARDINE IS not just one of the most numerous fish in the world, it's also one of the most important. It's a major part of so many food chains that you'd think it would be more in its interest to live alone – but that would go against the sardine's natural sociability.

Fecund familiarity

However, the familiar name of 'sardine' is misleading; the term is a more generic name for several small, shoaling sea fish that form some of the greatest aggregations of animals on Earth – not bad for a group of fish that grow no bigger than 20 cm (8 in). From storm-battered seas off the Cape of Good Hope in South Africa to the sun-drenched surf of the Mediterranean, what we call 'sardines' come in many guises – as we will now find out.

As far as my illustration is concerned, sardine is a synonym for European pilchard – one of the most

The name is rather old and is used almost indiscriminately about most small and silvery fish.

numerous and widely commercially exploited of the species under the sardine banner. The small fish we call 'sardines' are different from anchovies, which is a catch-all name for about 140 species in the family Engraulidae. Anchovies often share the same waters as sardines, but their lineage separated from their less salty distant relatives approximately 100 million years ago.

Three genera share the name sardine: *Sardinops*, *Sardina* and *Sardinella*. Similar fish also dubbed with the name sardine are distributed through global oceans, from Japan to South America, through California to South Africa. The one thing the members of the family all have in common is their affinity for cooler water temperatures between 14–20°C (57–68°F), and so are largely found in temperate regions.

The etymology of the name 'sardine' comes from the fact that they were commonly caught around Sardinia, off the coast of Italy. Others say the name comes from the resemblance of the species' reddish flesh to a red gemstone found in Europe known as sard. Either way, the name is rather old and is used almost indiscriminately about most small and silvery fish – at least they are all similar looking and related! Even the United Nations' Fishery and Agriculture Organization recognizes twenty-one species under this term.

From the food chain to the plate

The humble sardine is important to us for several reasons. They provide us with valuable food in massive quantities, and are rich

in proteins, vitamins, minerals and omega-3 fatty acids. Above all, though, sardines are a vital part of the ocean's food chain, turning the base nutrients into energy-packed small fish. Sardines also play a huge role in human societies, both culturally and commercially. Sardine oil is used in paints, varnish and even engine oil. Overall, sardines can be seen to have a significantly positive impact on human life in general. However, like many things that benefit in nature, we seem to have been rather bad at understanding that until it is almost too late.

Sardines form some of the densest shoals of fish in the world.

Cannery Row in Monterey Bay, California – made famous in John Steinbeck's book of the same name – was a thriving industry, employing thousands of people all for one reason: to put sardines into cans. The local Californian sardine population could be measured in its billions. The deep upwellings from the Farallon Trench and Monterey Canyon, which almost touch the coast, are cold and rich with nutrients – perfect for immense shoals of these tiny foraging fish. A huge industry sprang up during the 1950s, which processed several million tons of sardines every year and an aggregated production line that produced huge numbers of tinned fish, a boon to employment – and a staggering amount of waste and smells, too. This important industry, which turned Monterey into one of the busiest fishing ports in the world, finally closed down on 15 April 2010 when the last cannery closed its doors forever, having hung on after every other factory had long shut. There were no more Californian sardines left to process and package; the cupboard was bare. This was a lesson in human greed, and sardines are currently protected by state law – and, if managed correctly, they may make a comeback. Sardines are tough and resilient.

The sardine bounces back

One of the most famous fishing events in the world – in fact, one of the greatest natural events – is the sardine run off the coast of South Africa. Between May and July, a regular shout goes out among fishermen: 'Here they come!' The waters of the Agulhas Current, which runs north from South Africa to Mozambique, turns black from the density of the shoals of Southern African pilchards (*Sardinops sagax*) after they begin moving northwards en masse. These single-species shoals often measure more than 7 km (4 miles) long, 1.5 km (almost 1 mile) wide and 30 m (100 ft) deep (a volume of 337.5 million m^2) – and can be visible from space. About twenty-five sardines can squeeze into 1 m^2, meaning that there could be up to 8,437.5 million sardines present.

These enormous shoals migrate along the coast towards Durban to their breeding grounds for spawning. The conditions have to be perfect. Every year, the cold southern Benguela Current pushes east and meets the warmer rich Agulha Current that flows down the eastern coast of Africa. The result is a creeping slab of cold water that allows the sardines to access the masses of food present in a nutrient-rich zone that is out of reach to them for the rest of the year.

The exact timing of this annual event is impossible to predict with any precision, as yet. One year could be record-breaking, while the next almost a non-event. For instance, 2020 was a great year but 2018 not so good. This amazing event attracts lots of tourists and there is a hotline to ring to find out the best place to go see the run that year. It also attracts an amazing variety of predators, starting with Cape gannets, followed by three or four species of dolphin – including bottlenoses and spinners – sharks, including the rare dusky shark, brown fur seals and whales, including the giant common Bryde's whale; no predator wants to miss out on this productive bonanza, particularly as the billions of fish that thicken the sea to a black soup can so suddenly disappear, dropping away into the cold depths.

Sardines form these enormous shoals to migrate along the coast.

49

EUROPEAN EEL

{Anguilla anguilla}

A.K.A.

Glass eel, yellow eel

SIZE

Male: 35 cm (14 in)
Female: 50 cm (20 in)

HABITAT

From freshwater rivers
to the Sargasso Sea

**DISTINGUISHING
FEATURES**

Snake-like body

PERSONALITY

Wanderer

LIKES

Being mysterious

SPECIAL SKILLS

Self-transformation

**CONSERVATION
STATUS**

Critically Endangered

ONE LONG-STANDING MYSTERY for naturalists was the apparent lack of young eels in their home rivers. Only fully grown eels ever seemed to be found, so how did they breed? And what about those other apparently different types of eel, called 'glass eels' and 'silver eels' – where did they fit in? These cryptic creatures, in fact, represented the different stages in an eel's life cycle, a story of transformation as remarkable the butterfly's.

Anguilla anguilla was first described in 1758 by Linnaeus himself – the father of all taxonomy. It wasn't until 1912 that Johannes Schmidt, a Danish naturalist, suggested that efforts to find the European eel's breeding grounds should be concentrated on the Sargasso Sea, an almost mythical, huge, but largely still area far out in the south-western Atlantic Ocean. The Sargasso Sea is a very strange place – a sea with no land borders (unlike the Caspian or Black Seas). It sits completely inside the Atlantic Ocean and is caused or created by the most perfect set of conditions. The Sargasso Sea is famous for its deep blue colour, amazing water clarity and the large quantities of *Sargassum* seaweed, after which it is named. Unfortunately, it is now also home to the North Atlantic garbage patch, which we'll discuss shortly.

Travels and transformations

From Scandinavia through Britain and across to Turkey, mature eels leave the rivers and waterways of Europe and migrate through thousands of miles of ocean to meet up and breed. Female eels can lay up to 10 million eggs, which are then left to float around at the whims of the (admittedly minimal) currents. It is likely that once the adults have spawned, they die – no adult fish have ever been recorded returning to their rivers of origin.

Once hatched, the first stage of the life cycle is the larval form or leptocephalus. This flat amoeba-like form of fry has teeth and looks like a leaf. The larvae lead a floating existence, eating a wide variety of drifting detritus and remain in this form for about a year, as they drift gradually closer to the European mainland. As they grow, they transform into what are known as 'glass eels' – mini-eels that are

The Sargasso Sea is a very strange place – a sea with no land borders.

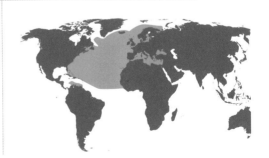

transparent: a pretty nifty disguise in open ocean. They are about to begin the second phase of their existence: life in freshwater. As they approach the coast, the tiny eels become elvers, gaining pigmentation as they home in on the estuaries and river mouths to begin their journeys upstream. The elvers are quite capable of climbing obstacles in their way, such as weirs and small dams – and to avoid predators they often do this at night in their hundreds, as otherwise it leaves them somewhat vulnerable. Once settled into this new freshwater world, they change once more, this time into what are called 'yellow eels' – so-called because they develop a yellow-tinged underside. This is the form with which we are most familiar.

The yellow eels spend between six and twenty years in their new home, eating, growing longer and thicker, intensifying their black and yellow pigmentation until, one day, they feel the itch to go travelling again. This is when they transform for the last time – into 'silver eels'. Not only do they become silver-coloured with white bellies, but also their eyes expand, their guts shrink, their skins thicken and even their fins enlarge so they can become better swimmers. The silver eels disappear from the rivers almost overnight, travelling by night again and heading out to the wide expanses of the open ocean. They navigate using an innate electromagnetic 'sixth sense' towards the sea with no borders, the Sargasso Sea. There, they meet up with thousands of other eels from all over Europe under the southern Atlantic sun to mix and spawn.

Eel farming is a fairly new but growing industry.

This complex and far-flung life cycle worked well for millennia, but its prolonged and seascape-scale naturally is also its weakness when things begin to go wrong. The European eel is now considered critically endangered by the IUCN. Its populations have fallen by 90–98 per cent – an appalling and catastrophic decline. By building huge dam walls for hydro-power schemes, we have reduced accessibility to many rivers. These monster constructions create deadly obstacles in the form of turbines that can literally chop eels to death. Overfishing has always made a massive impact on population numbers – as not only do we eat the adults, we collect the glass eels for fertilizers and other mundane uses.

European eels can live for fifty years, longer in captivity.

Plastic whirlpool

Then there is pollution. The North Atlantic garbage patch floating in the Sargasso Sea – effectively a huge raft of discarded industrial and domestic plastic waste – blocks out light and changes the water temperature, making much of the region unsuitable for breeding eels and other threatened animals such as turtles. The eels are also highly susceptible to microplastics, which poison them or take up room in their stomachs essential for digesting food. Even subtler chemical killers, such as PCBs (polychlorinated biphenyl – a dioxin) and the infamous DDT, poison the fish, too.

Conservationists, the fishing industry and the general public are all very concerned about this decline in what is surely an iconic fish species. The Sustainable Eel Group is just one organization that has been set up to help save this species. Eel farming is a fairly new but growing industry, but reproducing all the conditions this complex species needs for it to successfully breed is a tough call. One trial study even put adult eels into swimming machines to help them feel like they were migrating. Despite this, we are only just beginning to find our way into sustainable approaches to put right the damage we've done to the European eel.

With such a fascinating life cycle, though, it's the least we can do.

50 | BLUE TILAPIA

{Oreochromis aureus}

A.K.A.

Blue kurper, Jordan St Peter's fish

SIZE

13–20 cm (5–8 in)

HABITAT

Wide range of freshwater streams, rivers, lakes and ponds

DISTINGUISHING FEATURES

Broad dorsal fin

PERSONALITY

Invasive

LIKES

Keeping their young in their mouths

SPECIAL SKILLS

Can tolerate high and low temperatures

CONSERVATION STATUS

Least Concern

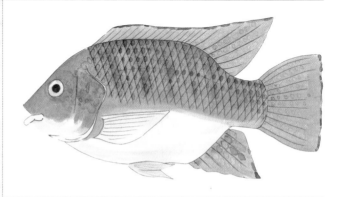

THERE ARE FEW fish that can boast that they have been eaten almost everywhere in the world – but the blue tilapia is one of the most farmed freshwater fish (perhaps second only to the salmon) and appears on more restaurant menus than any other.

In reality, not all 'blue tilapia' are blue tilapia. This seemingly exotic name is often used as a catch-all for many species of fish from the Cichlidae family that are farmed, caught and eaten across the world. The real blue tilapia is native to North and West Africa and the Middle East, having made the leap across the Red Sea to Israel. It is one of the many species of cichlid – a large and complex family – that inhabits the myriad lakes and rivers of that mighty continent. Cichlids have some distinctive habits that set them apart from other fish. One such trait peculiar to tilapia (a name that covers most of the 100 species of cichlid and is shared among six different tribes) in particular is the habit of brooding the young in the mouth.

A world in a lake

In the cosmopolitan world of a large African lake, where every species is busy carving out their own niche, some will be specializing in consuming different kinds of plants and animal, with some even surviving by eating other fish's fins or eyes (a niche perfect for Halloween). In such competitive circumstances, it pays to come up with novel ways to eat and to look after your young in order to ensure the continued success of your genetic line. To be able to do this, tilapia keep their young in their mouths – well away from more predatory mouths. The female tilapia avoid eating their own young by generating a combination of hormones and steroids to suppress their appetites while they are mouthbrooding.

The blue tilapia appears on more restaurant menus than any other.

Tilapia are certainly not the only fish to pull this trick off (other mouthbrooders including the arowana mentioned on pages 152–5), but so successful is this method that it makes them perfect fish to raise in captivity. Because they keep their babies close to their chests, owners don't have to repeatedly separate the fry from their parents like you do with some other fish that seem hell bent on destroying their own kind. However, mouthbrooding is not the only trick that has made these cichlids perfect for world domination.

Salt and heat

These hardy fish can thrive in a wide range of temperatures; their optimal 'sweet spot' is at around 27.8–30°C (82–86°F), but they can cope with temperatures as low as 12°C (54°F) although, at this point, they start becoming more susceptible to disease and parasites. They are able to live happily in very dense populations, but obviously this impacts their growth and hygiene. They are also able to cope with a wide range of salinities. This robustness is really important in keeping captive individuals in the artificial world of an aquarium – if the tank's filter stops working or the thermostat breaks, tilapia can cope, for a while at least. Their plant-based diet also helps them conserve the energy often expended rapidly by obligate hunters.

Blue tilapia are farmed all over the world in at least 125 countries. Huge vats of these attractive metallic green and gold fish are maintained in industrialized 'farms', making them the most prolific domestically farmed fish. Tilapia play a key role in feeding people in undeveloped countries, whose daily protein intake might otherwise be very limited. Breeding the mammals that western countries are so reliant upon, such as cows and sheep, takes lots of valuable time and land and is ultimately not very efficient. Farming tilapia removes all that stress and has been practised for a long time.

It is not possible to prove which species of fish Jesus Christ fed the famous 'five thousand' in the Bible story, but they were highly likely to have been tilapia. Blue tilapia are found in the river Jordan in Israel and are frequently referred to as the St Peter's Fish, owing to another story from the Gospel of Matthew, in which St Peter caught a fish with a coin in its mouth. The species is native to the Middle East as

The tilapia has an eye-catching shimmery blue-green colour.

well as Africa, and many of the ancestors of the world's farmed tilapia probably originated from Israeli stock. Although blue tilapia is clearly a useful food resource around the globe, it can also be a nuisance.

Dramatic introduction

Alien species are a real environmental and commercial concern, as we saw with the goldfish and sea lamprey, and our habitual taking of animals from faraway places and introducing them to parts of the world where they don't belong is constantly causing new problems in all regions of the world. Other culprits that I have already touched upon include red lionfish and brown trout, and blue tilapia are one of the prolific invasive aliens among fish, too.

Invasive populations of blue tilapia are now well established throughout the southern USA, where conditions are clearly perfect for it. It eats algae, making it a useful and handy addition to any aquarist's collection by cutting down on cleaning. However, the USA has its own natural eaters of algae, such as largemouth bass (*Micropterus salmoides*) and some freshwater mussel in the family Unionidae, and numbers of these native animals have been greatly reduced in Florida and Texas respectively by the presence of blue tilapia. This tough cichlid is spreading and is implicated in declines in the populations of many other plants, invertebrates and fish. Its tenacious breeding and dispersal behaviours have implicated it in deleterious structural changes in some large lakes' entire fish communities, causing a great deal of commercial and ecological damage as they overwhelm and out-compete native fish. As they are also farmed in Brazil, India and China, and frequently escape or are set free by unwitting owners, there may be no end to the damage tilapia might do.

Blue tilapia is one of the prolific invasive aliens among fish.

However, this impact couldn't really be called the fault of the fish. It is just too good at surviving in so many environments to be anything but a success almost anywhere.

Index

First published in 2021 by Ivy Press,
an imprint of The Quarto Group.
The Old Brewery, 6 Blundell Street
London, N7 9BH, United Kingdom
T (0)20 7700 6700 F (0)20 7700 8066
www.QuartoKnows.com

ISBN 978-0-7112-6099-3

10 9 8 7 6 5 4 3 2 1

Typeset in Dante MT
Design by Rosamund Bird

Printed in Singapore

MIX
Paper from
responsible sources
FSC™ C007207

Photographic credits

12 Ganjar Rahayu / 500px / Getty Images; 16 wildestanimal / Getty Images; 21 Georgette Douwma / Getty Images; 24 bekirevren / Shutterstock; 29 Boris Bulychev / Shutterstock; 33 Shane Gross / Shutterstock; 37 Mark Newman / Getty Images; 42 nickeverett1981 / Shutterstock; 47 Paulo Oliveira / Alamy Stock Photo; 51 Pavaphon Supanantananont / Shutterstock; 55 David Shale / Nature Picture Library; 58 David Fleetham / Alamy Stock Photo; 62 isoft / Getty Images; 67 Alessandro Mancini / Alamy Stock Photo; 70 Tier Und Naturfotografie J und C Sohns / Getty Images; 75 beto_junior / Shutterstock; 80 Danny Ye / Shutterstock; 85 Stephen Frink Collection / Alamy Stock Photo; 88 Doug Mackay Hope; 92 Juan Jose Napuri Guevara / 500px / Getty Images; 96 Paulo Oliveira / Alamy Stock Photo; 101 Vincent Jary / Getty Images; 105 John Back / Shutterstock; 111 Paul Starosta / Getty Images; 115 Minakryn Ruslan / Shutterstock; 118 Smithlandia Media / Getty Images; 122 Nature Picture Library / Alamy Stock Photo; 127 YAY Media AS / Alamy Stock Photo; 130 Martin Strmiska / Alamy Stock Photo; 137 Paulo Oliveira / Alamy Stock Photo; 140 Cherdchai Chaivimol / Shutterstock; 145 Nate Abbott / Getty Images; 149 BioStock Images / Alamy Stock Photo; 152 Anthony Pierce / Alamy Stock Photo; 157 Kris Wiktor / Shutterstock; 160 Cavan Images / Getty Images; 167 ivSky / Shutterstock; 171 feathercollector / Shutterstock; 174 left agefotostock / Alamy Stock Photo; 174 right Maria Dryfhout / Shutterstock; 179 WaterFrame / Alamy Stock Photo; 183 Paulo Oliveira / Alamy Stock Photo; 186 Biosphoto / Alamy Stock Photo; 191 Paulo Oliveira / Alamy Stock Photo; 195 Rostislav Stefanek / Shutterstock; 201 David Higgins / Alamy Stock Photo; 204 Rich Carey / Shutterstock; 209 Roberto Nistri / Alamy Stock Photo; 212 Jao Cuyos / Shutterstock; 217 Nature Photographers Ltd / Alamy Stock Photo; 220 Christian Vinces / Shutterstock.